Universe On the Move

9/20/2009 = 11 11

Tara A. Rae

Dearst Deb
thank you for opening to
the wholeness of The Universe
your movement has
begun.
Love ~ Tara Rae

Angel Heart Publishing
Houston, Texas
713-784-7440

ISBN 0-9671872-0-6

Second Printing July 2000

Cover illustration by Arthur Douét

Printed in the United States of America.

Published by
Angel Heart Publishing
Houston, TX
713-784-7440

Acknowledgements

Special thanks to:

Mario, a wonderful talented and helpful woman who took the stories that I recorded on tapes and transcribed them into a story-telling manuscript, who also spent countless hours in formatting the mock-up copies.

Jane Davis, who guided me on my business trips out West and returned me to my career in nutrition. Also for creating various graphics on her delicious Apple.

Concessions International - NW Edition - for having enough faith in my book to sell in their stores at Sea-Tac Airport.

Brocky Brown of Brockton Publishing Company who enjoys helping me help others.

Indigo Sun Magazine, Carol Money, Ginger McCord and Ruth Money for my first pre-publishing party and the use of a laptop.

Carole Franklin Ph.D., applied linguist and college professor of English, for lending me her wee MacPlus so I could type and revise the manuscript myself, instead of asking others.

Shirley MacLaine, for coming out of the Metaphysical closet, by writing and talking on subjects not yet fashionable in the year *Out On A Limb* also came out.

International Group Cruises (Silva Cruises), 800-638-6000 ex. 307. Thanks, Victor, for my overdue trip to Mexico.

Foreword

Tara Rae, an intuitive spiritual Lightworker, has come to Earth during this time of enlightenment to teach herself and others "how to be all you can be, without joining the Army." She has explained this as, *"If it's not easy and effortless, don't do it. If it doesn't feel good in your heart, your adult barometer, don't do it at all!"*

Her stories are so alive that you will feel compelled to read on and on just to find out what she reveals next.

I have not known Tara long, but have had the honor of having her as a house guest whenever we work together at Whole Life Expos and Conventions. When I am with her, I have noticed that no matter how tired her physical body is, she always has the energy to make herself accessible to all who ask for help. She once told me that when she was twelve, she was taught how to use many forms of Eastern and intuitive modalities of healing, through the guidance of The Universe, her Guides and Teachers. Tara has said she cannot use these techniques unless she is asked for help and they are ready to get on with their life. Just by standing next to you, she knows what part of your body is in disharmony.

I've watched as she freely talks at length to anyone who walks up to her and says, "I have a pain in my body," "My life is a mess, can you help me?" or when she is explaining how to use gemstones and minerals as tools for the body. I asked her how these people knew she was skillful at healing them. She answered me by saying, "It seems my energy field, which gives out a familiar vibration, allows them to know I can help. I believe it may be this same energy field and God-given intuition, that permitted people to seek out and follow Jesus." Tara went on to say, "Everyone is capable of doing what I do. God did not say, 'Only Jesus will do my work on Earth.' He sent many Lightworkers to Earth, but not all have realized their missions yet." When I asked her why she does not teach on a stage in front of the masses as others do, she explained to me that she is on the lecture circuit but prefers to be at a table or booth to make it easier for those seeking her out. This way she has easier access to touch more in the way Jesus did.

The real thing I love about Tara, is Tara. She refuses to listen to small talk or gossip. When having a conversation with her, she jumps right to the heart of the matter and helps you to get in touch with the truth of the problem. She is always in the moment; when she brings you into that space with her, you realize that you have missed so much in your life by living in the past and dragging all your old memories around with you. Tara will help stop this process instantly and throw that unresolved moment back in your face so you can *deal with it and let it go*. When people first meet her, they do not know whether to hug her or slap her. Later, when they realize what she says was true and for their Highest Good, they are ready to hug her. Sometimes, you have to try hard to stop crying or laughing during your encounter with her. She is powerful in her own right and is capable of helping others tune into the powers given to them by Divine Right.

Thank you Tara, for being in my life and for showing me how my mission will be more enjoyable.

Jane Davis
Entrepreneur and Mother

Table of Contents

Introduction

"The Universal Wholeness" which we are born into and consciously choose before we come to Earth, is always with us, guiding us. This book is a collection of personal journeys and inspirational stories as told to me by clients and those I have met during my travels. I have learned to bless and recognize coincidences, The Universal Miracles, as signs from an unseen "Wholeness." I have also come to understand that Angels, Guides, Teachers, the Holy Spirit, God, and Jesus are always working to guide us in discovering our true purpose and goals. You will come to see, that as I recognized and honored each coincidence, my purpose to heal others emerged. I believe this process reflects the truth for all of us as we begin to notice and affirm that we are indeed part of the "Universal Love Flow," as we grow into Wholeness and live our rightful purpose, *which is ours by Divine Right.*

When is it time to get on with your life? The time is now!
I look into people's eyes and tell them their stuff without sugar coating it, which is why I am known as a Butt-kicking Angel. I also do not see clients in an on-going fashion. *"Giving you the tools to get on with your own life"* is my motto. I once heard a lecturer say, "Jesus was a Butt-kicking Angel." This was evident when he overturned the tax tables; blasting the workers of Rome for insulting their synagogues by conducting their unholy practices. I also relate to Jesus for healing those who traveled to meet him; I am happy to be in such good company.

Those who have made a soul connection with me, knew in their heart, the adult barometer, that one session or class was enough to help awaken their unconscious mind to an unseen world, thus leading them to be all they can be.

Faith and trust have always brought me to the correct answers, people, and places because I am living in the right time and place; the Aquarian age, my chosen birth sign. It is also safe to trust and use my God-given powers for the Higher Good of all concerned.

"Have faith, and trust in the Divine"

My desire, as you read these stories, is to inspire you and I ask you to remember the times when you uttered, "What a miracle!" or "How could that have happened to me?" I ask you to consider this: Sweet Spirit (God's Universal Light and Wisdom) is The Universal Wholeness, we never lose and are always connected to. We also have the gift of free will, therefore, "The Grand Omnipotent Energy Force" is not at liberty to help us unless we ask. Remember our most holy instructions, *"Ask, and it shall be given to you; seek, and ye shall find; knock, and it shall be opened unto you."* Matthew 7:7. K.J.V.

Our souls know their true purpose when we come to Earth on our special birthday, but the dross, Earth's negative electromagnetic energy, hypnotizes us and we forget our true purpose. One day, when we allow ourselves to re-connect to our God-given powers, *we remember.* For me, it happened the day I turned my head upward and shouted, "I've had enough! Show me a better way!" Since that day, I have taken giant steps to be all I can be. I have been shown miraculous and wonderful ways to lead my life and to help others enjoy theirs to the fullest. I began by traveling from coincidence to coincidence and moving on to healing after healing. I believe my growth in Wholeness may inspire you — so, come with me on a journey and begin to remember how sacred and connected we all are!

"When you remember what you were brought here to do, you will then do what you want to, and be Who you want to be."

Welcome all, to Earth 101; the greatest classroom toward enlightenment!

"Love is the way I walk in Gratitude."

Chapter 1

My Life Story

In the beginning...
I believe I chose a Jewish family because I made a soul conscious decision to be born into the same faith Jesus was when He walked upon the Earth as a healer of men.

From kindergarten and throughout high school and college, I did not bond with my peers or teachers because I felt their lack of spiritual oneness and connection with body, mind and soul. I still feel that way today. I preferred to be with adults than those closer to my age, which allowed me to learn more about life. I was deeply offended when Atheist Madeleine Murray O'Hare was instrumental in pushing the U.S. Supreme Court into taking religion, especially the Lord's Prayer, out of all government school systems. After the decision was implemented, I felt our society lost the essence of Sweet Spirit.

When you say or sing The Lord's Prayer, it creates what I call a "Chaktavation" or the activation of the Chakras; a Vortex of energy that runs down your spinal column. When you finish speaking or singing those powerfully inspiring words, you will experience a sense of peace as you become one with The Universe.

School bored me. I intuitively knew there was something more to learn in life than the school's philosophies. I also sensed that most of the curriculum lacked the important information that would be helpful to me in this lifetime. I wanted to learn how to be a better human being, how to be a good parent, how to stay in my power and be all I can be, and how to love and feel good about myself, or as author John Bradshaw states in his lectures, "Love yourself enough to love others more."

I often wondered if Jesus, because He was so special, ever had feelings of separateness as I felt growing up.

I enjoy learning from the school of "God-knocks," as opposed to the school of hard-knocks.

"When you are through being part of the school of 'hard-knocks,' join the school of "God-knocks" and all will be opened unto you."

Enlightenment through illness

I was sickly until my late 20's. In fact, it was easier for me to remain ill than to be well. Now, I realize that I chose this unpleasant situation by creating a constant "poor-me syndrome." I received much-wanted attention from doctors, nurses and therapists, because I never felt the attention I wanted from my parents or anyone else.

Every summer, my parents rented a bungalow in the Catskill Mountains located in upstate New York. The summer I was 12, I was caught in a heavy downpour and developed a 105 degree fever. No matter how large the dose of antibiotics the doctors pumped into me, the fever would not break. Finally, after a week, the fever suddenly broke. Although I do not consciously remember everything that transpired during what I felt was a near-death experience, I do feel that The Universe needed to put me into a near-coma state in order to teach me, *in their high speed way,* what I would need to know in order to fulfill my life's purpose —*to be a Healer!*

A second, near-death experience occurred when I was in my early 20's, again while visiting the Catskills. I had met a musician there and believed when I returned we could continue the relationship. He was busy and palmed me off, I felt, on a friend named Ray. I went to Ray's apartment and he fixed what appeared to be a harmless glass of orange juice. After I drank it, I realized it contained more than just orange juice when I started to feel dizzy. When I asked him what was in it he said he added methadone so we both could get high. (I found out later that Methadone is a synthetic heroine widely used to help recovering addicts during withdrawal.) This harmless looking concoction caused an allergic reaction, where I was going in and out of consciousness. He kept shaking me; attempting to keep me awake, but I kept telling him to, "Leave me alone; just let me sleep." I remember a warm peaceful feeling taking me over that I did not want to end. When my breathing became labored, he was terrified that something was terribly wrong, so he rushed me to the nearest hospital. If Ray had left me alone, I would have died.

Later, on one of his many visits to the hospital, Ray told me while he was deciding what to do, he heard a strong voice telling him to take me with great speed to the nearest facility for help or I would surely die! He said upon hearing that, he quickly drove me to a hospital that had been converted from a large house; the only healing facility in a fifty mile radius. There were no doctors and only one nurse on duty that night. After placing me on an examining table, he ran to a pay phone and called his doctor who gave him the name of the antidote. He returned to the nurse and gave her this information. By then I had stopped breathing completely! Ray told me the nurse stood there looking over my body and angrily asked him, "How did you know to use Naline; are you a doctor?" He said that he was not a doctor but since she did not know what to do, and it was obvious I was in trouble, she had nothing to lose. So Ray told her to give me the medicine.

Thankfully, she did. Within seconds, I opened my eyes and looked down at my disheveled dress realizing that it was the same one I had worn that evening. I asked the nurse in a slow, sleepy voice, "Where am I?" The rotund lady in white replied, "You're in the hospital!" I again returned to unconsciousness.

I was kept in the hospital three days while I detoxified. When I was first brought to the hospital, I had episodes where I felt as if I was floating out of my body. I was awakened to the knowledge that I did not leave this life because I still had important work to do.

Although I no longer dwell on my toxic past, I share with you the final affliction that occurred when I was in my late 20's. This physical ailment, with deep emotional ties, showed me I was able to live a much more fulfilling life when I allowed myself to release the emotions causing my problems in the first place.

I suffered from a troubled gall bladder, the organ that represents the emotion of being stuck. That is how I felt at the time —

stuck in a body, a job, and a life I disliked. I did not have a clue at the time what I wanted to do. In fact, I did not like any job I held; I would quit or continuously be released from my obligations during those transitional years. However, the day I had my gall bladder removed, there was a completion of sorts, and the subconscious emotional ties that represented my being stuck vanished. During my recuperation, I looked up to the sky and shouted, *"That's it! I've had enough! Show me a better way!"* The moment I spoke those liberating words, I felt an uplifting freedom the likes of which I had never felt before. It was as though,

> *"There was an unknown force within me, waiting for a spark to ignite the wisdom that would be my life's work."*

At last, I was free to head onto a completely different path one towards a life of enlightenment filled with Love and Light. I was guided to read three books that laid the cornerstone of the new life I was to lead, which in itself was interesting since I am not much of a reader. The first was, *How to Be Well*, on the use of vitamins by Adele Davis. The second was, *Back to Eden*, an herb book by Jethro Kloss and the third was, *How to Get Well*, combining vitamins, herbs and food nutrition by Paavo Ariola. After reading these books, I understood that, **"Change was necessary!"**

> *"Healing the past is necessary to fulfill your destiny."*

After releasing the dis-ease within my body, mind and spirit, I now felt guided to live a more empowered and happy life; as we are all brought to Earth to do.

Looking back on my two near-death experiences in the Catskills, I realized a correlation was emerging, especially after I remembered another incident in my early teens when a tree barely missed me during a hurricane. With the knowledge of this third incident, it was enough to warrant an explanation. I asked guidance as to why I kept going back to a place that was trying to kill me! The answer was, "During these experiences as an unhappy child, you were returning to the place where you felt you never received the love and attention you needed. Once again, you were using the only way you knew how in order to receive attention, and that was when you were sick. Therefore, as a lonely child you continued to return to the Catskills — even if it killed you!" After hearing those life altering words, I recalled that living in New York consisted mostly of physical and emotional pain, loneliness and a multitude of unhappy jobs and relationships.

It was not until I left for Florida and college, that I began looking for the reasons and answers to the question why my life was in such turmoil. I felt going back to my parents could be the place to start, since I found no resolution in therapy. My decision turned out to be correct and my return provided an abundant source of knowledge towards helping me to see clearly what had initially created my unwanted patterns. My lack of answers was quite apparent due to numerous past jobs and unfulfilled relationships.

A pattern that comes to mind when I blamed my father had to do with waiting for somebody to be there and to listen to me. Growing up, I did not see my father as much as I would have liked. Since he worked so much, I surmised he was a workaholic. Dad did not eat with the family because he came home late most nights. Since Mom was not much of a talker and was always cleaning something or another, I often ate alone with the television for company (I still do). When Dad came home after a 12 hour work day, he would eat, go straight to his favorite recliner, smoke a cigarette, and fall asleep in front of the television.

Looking back, I understand that my father preferred to be at work where he must have felt more appreciated than coming home to a family that complained about the lack of money, among other things. Once, I asked Mom why she thought we did not have enough money. She claimed that Dad gave too much away to relatives and extended credit to customers because, she said, everyone knew he was an easy touch. What bothered her the most was she felt that he gave family money away without discussing it with her first. This established her feelings that everybody else came first, which created the same feelings in my life.

I remember once, when finances were tight, having to plead with my relatives to stop asking my Dad for money he did not have, as my mother had done to no avail. I understand now, Dad felt compelled to lend money to them, or anything else they needed because he received pleasure whenever he did; an emotion he must have needed, if he felt he did not get it at home.

This behavior is a form of buying people's affection or friendship. Copying my father, again, seemed to be a way of life for me. I once asked my father, why, even with a successful business, did we never have any money. He confided in me that he discovered his two partners stealing and he knew that he had no choice but to buy them out. He said he was in a quandary as to where he would find the money needed to make that possible; the banks would not lend him the money. Dad believed he had no other choice but to borrow it from a loan shark. Dad looked relieved after sharing his well kept secret. For too many years, most of his money went to pay off a high interest loan. Dad said he did not tell Mom because she would have worried. What Mom thought was useless spending on Dad's part, paid for a business that kept a roof over our heads even if it did not seem like it at the time.

I share this intimate story because it shows how sometimes we think we know what is going on within a family or any relationship, but not everything is as it seems in the 'Naked City.' This taught me never to jump to conclusions or presume anything.

"There are unknown hidden stories calling for explanations within our family madness."

Another copied pattern consisted of pleasing and buying people with gifts and money, just as I watched my father do. I knew that *my mimicking behavior had to stop!*

Behavior, where you obsessively seek love and acceptance, happens between yourself and anyone else you feel the overwhelming need to please. Although these attempts are not reciprocated, you still knock yourself out feeding this need; it seeps into a pleasing frenzy with all your relationships. Everyone you meet will remind you of the person you believe you were never able to please. No matter how much you want to please, it will never be enough, and you will develop the misperception "every time I open my heart, I will be hurt."

Understanding the cause and effect of all my emotional unhealthy experiences, contributed greatly toward a comprehensive change in my life. Releasing negative attitudes created a vacuum which allowed The Universe to respond in kind, and bestowed on me many useful attributes: becoming more in tune with my intuitive healing powers, unblocking my creativity and becoming more productive.

My gifts became even more apparent when I placed my hands on people and animals or was in their presence, such as the time when I visited a bookstore in California.

I met the manager of the store and I asked her if I could work there for the weekend while I was in town. When she asked what I did, I told her I was a healer. She wanted me to demonstrate on the pain in her back. I told her after I had lunch I would be happy to help her. When I returned, she said that as soon as I left, the pain was gone!

That day in the bookstore, I realized I did not have to touch anyone in order to help them because the healing energy from Sweet Spirit runs through me and is transmitted outwardly through my Aura.

Life with Dad and Mom

I believe that we choose our parents before we are born. I chose my father for his wonderful sense of humor and business savvy. Even though he was illiterate, he knew by memory and color, his entire product line in his grocery store. This proved to me that you do not need a college degree to be all you can be. My Dad was a self-made man with a degree in intelligence and common sense quickly learned through necessity.

I chose my Mother for her warm smile, commitment for keeping the family together no matter what, and the importance of independence. My parents were good people doing the best they could, but I could not rid myself from the imprints of toxic energy that I felt.

Toxic energy represents our earliest violent memories which, once imprinted, *always* remains within the mind. In order for these imprints to no longer impact your life, you must learn to understand and surrender them to where they can no longer influence and run your life, leaving you powerless. I was told by a friend of Timothy Leary, that L.S.D. was created for the purpose of removing our painful imprints and not the cult drug used solely for entertainment.

I learned to adapt to the negative feelings that fed the embers which kept me stuck most of my life: Nobody liked me. Nothing I did was ever good enough. Along with these beliefs I started feeling that I was fated to stay stuck in a life I hated. It was easier to blame my parents for all my ongoing difficulties, instead of getting in touch with my feelings.

Needing attention constantly crept into my life, creating a pattern of waiting for people to decide my fate. Like waiting for the phone to ring when someone said they would call and did not; dates either showed up late or not at all, or someone promising they would do something and not follow through.

I chose to obsess and sulk instead of opening to and understanding the legitimate cause of why these feelings occurred. One of the reasons I felt this way was, I had convinced myself that I was unlovable. This pattern is still with me today; I continue to attract those who do not follow through with what they promised, setting me up for disappointment, but only if I allow it. This is one way we sabotage our lives when we have not healed our issues from the past. *It's all a set-up! "If we do not heal the past, we will most certainly repeat it."* Consequently, when I am with someone that I feel is not meeting my needs or expectations, I revert back to the old "poor-me" feelings.

Another one of my emotionally created distortions is that I feel I do not fit in, creating the feeling that I have nothing to say. One day I asked Sweet Spirit, "Why doesn't anyone listen to me?" I was gently told, "When you have something to say, they will listen." Today that statement is true. When I come from my Higher Self and not from my past traumatic stress syndromes, people listen with open hearts and minds to what comes forth.

Dad

My father's three pack a day cigarette habit was a constant source of irritation to my mother. Mom was always yelling, "Jack, put your cigarette out! One of these days you are going to burn us all up in our sleep!" This addiction led to emphysema. To this day, I am a light sleeper, due to the fear of dying in my sleep.

The terminally ill know when they are ready to die

Mom and Dad retired and moved to Florida from New Jersey in the early 1970's. Three years later I decided to join them. Dad did not have much time left and I wanted to be with him. In my heart I knew it was time to heal the unhappy memories disturbing me before it was too late. I also used this opportunity to finally attend college in order to find out if I missed anything by not continuing my education after high school and small private schools.

Dad spent a lot of time in the hospital because of the emphysema. Every time he came home, he appeared weaker and was soon in a wheelchair using oxygen almost full-time. The final trauma to his body happened when he was getting severe pains in the liver area and was told his only recourse was to have his gall bladder removed. (Sound familiar? Seems like stuckness was his pattern too!) I offered to help him by naturally removing the stones, since I felt surgery was a drastic maneuver. However, Dad wanted a quick cure, so it was easy for the doctor to talk him into surgery. I explained to his doctor that sometimes surgery is not the best remedy for the severely ill. He refused to listen to any of my suggestions and put my father in harm's way. To my surprise and due to Dad's strong constitution, he came through it. The surgery was the final assault on an already weakening life force and it took its toll. While Dad was recuperating, Mom called and said that he wanted to come home before the doctor felt it was time. Dad knew it was his time and wanted to die in his own bed. The evening he returned home, Mom asked me if I wanted to stay the night. I refused because somewhere in my heart, I knew it was his time and part of me did not want to see him go. My intuition was correct and he died early the next morning.

After Dad died, I felt I went through a symbolic death of my own. Like Dad, I was always sick and his death acted as a wake-up call for me. It was time to open to the answers that I waited so long for. Although my inner child would have liked to let them die with Dad, the adult me knew that was not realistic, if I was to heal and grow strong. I chose the day of his funeral to find out my answers. I asked "Why, while growing up, did I continue to be sick?" The answer was, "You chose to believe that your father was not there for you most of your life. Being sick, just like the father you loved, was the only feasible way to feel closer to him. This brought you emotional peace of mind, but a body always in dis-ease."

"Disease is the physical body in emotional dis-ease. When you do not get in touch and release emotional problems, they will manifest into physical disease."

A year after Dad died, he appeared to me in a solid state, unlike what we are use to seeing in the movies, in the room I was staying in at my parents' condo. He sat down next to me and with an unusually smiling face told me all the things he was unable to say when he was alive. He said that he always loved me and that he was sorry that he was not able to show it or be more verbal in his love in the way I needed. At his funeral, I became aware of my problems but it was not until my father returned that one last time, did I release any residual negative energy remaining towards him. His visit provided me with a wonderful cleansing and I never felt as close to him as I did that miraculous day.

Considering his cold father, I truly understood that Dad loved me in the only way he was capable of. He learned by observing his parents, who showed more of a materialistic love than a verbal one. Dad's learned behavior helped to manifest a home without the (preferred) hugs.

Since there are no schools on how to be perfect parents, the only way we learn is to listen and watch first hand, our significant role model adults around us. I remember my Grandfather, born in war-torn Poland, being a distant man who chose not to speak English. Sadly, the bond to his grandchildren was unable to be achieved, perpetuating my feelings of distance with him as I am sure my father felt growing up. Having this kind of detached Grandfather helped me to understand how Dad would also be incapable of communicating love or receiving it. I also felt this loss with my Grandmothers, because they both died when I was around three. Mom told me that after her Mother died, I ran through the apartment halls screaming, "Grandma, where are you?" I do not consciously remember this action or my grandmothers in general, but to this day, I feel a sadness in my heart over losing them. I wonder what my life would have been like if they both had taken part in my up-bringing. *But then again it does not matter; everything happens for a reason.*

Mom

Mom was a Gemini who lived up to the twin persona. I remember her as being either happy or sad but nothing in between. Before Dad got sick with emphysema, he was a rageaholic. One day after one of his loud blow-ups, I asked Mom why she stayed and tolerated his verbal abuse. She said she did it for me and my sister.

I remember a time when my father came home from work and dinner was not completely on the table so he threw everything on the floor. I felt so sorry for my Mother as I watched, in shock, as she got down on her knees, silently picking up the ruined dinner. The next day I asked her if she ever thought of leaving Dad. She said that she had when I was an infant. Her sister, Eva, told her that she would take us both in if she would leave my father. Mom had reminded my Aunt that they were taught to keep the family together no matter what, so, she would not leave.

In the 1950's it was considered taboo for a family to break up, for any reason. I feel if a family unit is not flourishing, end it. It was not until I looked back, with an open heart and not with judgment, that I realized keeping our family together showed her to be stronger than I would have been if I 'walked a mile in her shoes.'

Children suffer from all the arguing, as I did. A year after my aunt suggested that Mom leave my father, my sister Barbara was born. Consequently, it was too late for Mom to break-away even if she decided to, because there was not enough room in my Aunt's two bedroom apartment with her husband and the three of us.

"Unresolved emotions create disease within the body."

My parents argued and I believe *seeing* this emotionally created the need at the early age of six for glasses. More than likely I no longer wanted to see my parents fight. Sure, poor eyesight could be caused by heredity or sitting too close to the TV, as some optometrists have told me, but not in my case, since neither of my parents wore glasses.

Mom never learned to drive. We rode the bus a lot and I remember one specific time when I wished she had learned how to drive. When I was about 13, I suffered from severe pain in my knees whenever I walked up and down the stairs. Mom took me to a clinic, which I found out later was for people who paid what they could afford. When we got there, I was poked and prodded by a room full of doctors because they were not sure how to treat my problem. The doctors diagnosed, after looking at the X-rays, that what *may be* causing my pain, *could be* due to the separation of the tibia and a secondary problem in which both knee caps were not centered properly. The doctors believed I was born with both problems. As part of the treatment, one doctor gave me an extremely painful injection in the right knee, the one having the worst separation. By not treating both knees at the same time, the cartilage in the left knee eventually tore; whereas my right knee is fine.

When we were ready to leave, I remember one doctor distinctly advising my mother to take me straight home or I would be in a lot of pain when the anesthetic wore off. Sometimes my mother seemed scattered and unfortunately, this was one of those times. Instead of taking me home, we went shopping; one of Mom's favorite past times. After what seemed like hours of endless shopping we caught the bus home. About five blocks from home, my knee began to hurt. By the time we got off, I was in excruciating pain. Thank God, a neighbor asked if we needed help. He carried me the two blocks from the bus stop and placed me on the living room couch. I was angry with my mother and blamed her for not taking proper care of me that day.

Since I am a strong advocate of "everything happens in Divine order," what happened during my recuperation period was worth the pain and anguish.

> *"No matter what we will learn and experience along life's highways and byways; everything happens in divine order."*

The treatment consisted of keeping the right leg immobile for six weeks in an uncomfortable, twelve pound thigh to ankle plaster cast. It was so heavy, I could not walk the school stairs. *Hooray, an excuse not to have to return to a school I did not enjoy!* To prevent my school work from suffering, so I could graduate, the school sent a tutor to my home. Mrs. Schwartz was a God-send. She was patient and loving, the two traits I felt were missing in most of my teachers. We worked on English, and she even made the ever unpopular math fun and easy. We even had time for another subject. When she asked me what else I would like to study, I happily said, "Music, please." Music was a favorite subject; I had been singing since the age of three to records in all my past life languages. *Coincidentally, she was also a music teacher*. This is an example of how The Universe included some fun along with the work.

"Even through adversity comes a Light to show the way."

Mom was not much of a hugger. In fact, I do not remember sharing much physical contact with her except when she taught me how to dance and when she took a part-time job in a candy factory. Her job seemed to give her the freedom she had not felt since before she was married. My father did not want my mother to work. He was brought up to believe that the wife stayed home and raised the children while the man provided. Every morning at 7:00 a.m. before leaving for work, she came into my room and hugged me good morning, along with a cheery good-bye and have a great day at school. On those days, Mom radiated with a glow of happiness I had not seen before.

Mom worked at Dad's store when we were teenagers, but she always told me how much she disliked it. I often watched as Dad became impatient and yelled unmercifully at her. When they moved to Florida, Mom acted as though she had been let out of prison. She made several new friends and had a great time while caring for my invalid father. After he died, you could hardly find Mom home. She lived her last seven years as if she were cramming an entire lifetime into it; going out to dinner with many male partners, taking cruises with her sister, seeing plays and lots of shopping. The only problem I saw with her choice of companions was they were all ailing. I told her she was a winning, outgoing woman and she could do so much better. She told me she learned all too well how to take care of the sick because of Dad (and probably me) so taking care of the sick was second nature to her.

I moved to Texas in 1983 from Florida and started a new life. One night I had a precognitive dream about Mom that bothered me the rest of the day. That evening, I telephoned my Aunt Eva, who lived a couple of condos away from Mom, and asked her if she had a key to Mother's condo. She reminded me that my Mom was too independent for her to give her a key. I asked her to please, get the house key anyway, because I had had a dream where Mom's door had to be broken down in order to get in.

The next day, my dream became a reality. Concerned about my dream, my aunt decided to check up on her sister; walking over to see how she was doing. That afternoon, she called and said what I dreamt had come true. She said she went to Mom's condo, knocked on the door and when Mom did not answer, she became worried and called the Fire Department. The firemen felt there was no time to go searching for a key, so they broke the door down. They found Mom in her bedroom sitting in her recliner. She was wearing her favorite house coat and staring straight at the door with her eyes wide open, like she was waiting for guests to arrive.

The next day, a friend drove me to the airport for the trip to Florida and Mom's funeral. On the way, we were delayed in traffic. Strangely, I was not upset, even with a strong chance of missing my plane. We arrived at the airport the same time the plane was scheduled to take off. I was fine until I walked inside and up to the departure video screens; realizing the worst had happened. I lost my composure and started screaming, "Oh God, I've missed my plane!" I turned to see a sky cap running toward me. He said that he heard me screaming and asked if he could be of assistance. I told him that my Mother had passed on and I was going to be late for her funeral. According to the monitor, the plane had already departed. He said he would check on the status of the plane, for which I thanked him. When he finished checking at the desk, he returned with great news. *The flight had been delayed!* With that, I left the terminal entrance and ran for the departure gate silently thanking The Universe, Mom or whomever, for keeping the plane on the ground so I would not miss it. When I arrived at the gate check-in counter, I felt compelled to give the obviously unhappy boarding attendant a big hug. She thanked me for the hug and told me she was glad someone was happy for this *unknown delay!* Within minutes of checking in, she announced, "Flight 242 to Ft. Lauderdale, Florida is now ready for departure." She turned to me and winked.

As soon as I entered Mom's condo, I took off my shoes just as I always do at home to create a sacred space. I started walking around when I had a flashback to when I was growing up, hearing Mom say, "Keep your shoes on in the house, I'm not dead yet. You only remove your shoes for the dead." (A Jewish tradition.) And "You could hurt your feet; put your shoes on!" Even after remembering what she said, I continued to walk around barefoot, when, as if on cue, I stubbed my toe. I jumped up and down as pain shot through my swelling big toe. Looking upward I said, "Okay, I'll wear my shoes while I'm in *your condo!* The usual, 'Put your shoes on before you hurt yourself' would have been sufficient to get my attention, today of all days!" I remembered another one of Mom's house rules, "This is my house and you will do what I say!" Talk about having the last word! That is what I call, *"Toeing the line!"*

I limped into Mom's bedroom where I found her legal papers sorted into neat piles on her bed. I also noticed a watch I had once coveted waiting for me on the dresser. When I first asked her for that watch years ago, she had said that I could have it when she was gone. I was so proud of her that day because she was truly in her power.

A week before, my sister had called and told me she was visiting Mom in the hospital. When I asked her why Mom was there, Barbara said she did not know. When I called Mom, I believed her when she said she was doing fine. A week later she was gone.

Although Mom was on medication for her diabetes and hypertension, her death was still unexpected. Since her death came as such a surprise, I decided to investigate her last day.

Mom visited many hair salons in the 15 years she lived in South Florida. When I found the correct shop, I asked her hair stylist how Mom looked when she arrived. She said that they had all wondered, seeing how sick she looked, how she found the strength to get out of bed much less walk there. Another operator said that she had done her nails and she also wanted a pedicure but it was obvious she was not feeling well. When I finished, I went back to Mom's bedroom, sat in her chair and intuitively pictured what she did after she returned home. Mom changed clothes, putting on her favorite housecoat, sat in her recliner, feeling happy after a day at the beauty salon, and faded into peaceful bliss — as Dad had seven years before in the same room.

Mom has never come back to visit me in a physical state as Dad has, but guides me in my dreams and on occasion calls out Audrey, the name she chose on the day of my birth. She told me Audrey was a name she heard on a radio soap opera just before I was born. Sometimes I hear Mom screaming out my name when I am shopping because she told me I always wandered away from her to find a water fountain or the bathroom. To this day I cannot go shopping without needing a drink or a trip to the toilet. Hearing Audrey alerts me that Mom is still watching over me.

Since Mom and Dad made their transition, my heart feels closer to them. Connecting through the Cosmos gives me a feeling that their spiritual energy is with me whenever I need it.

I came up with an analogy that I feel best describes my parents: *Mom and Dad were like uncut gems, maybe not as perfect as the quality of a faceted, finished stone; but to me, the beholder, as perfect and clear as they could be in their own Light.*

There are ongoing trials and tribulations that I will continue to live through, learn and understand, due to a profound awareness that has allowed me to grow healthy and whole, hence, leading me to become a more productive, enlightened person. After all, the learning never stops.

During a hairdressing appointment, we were discussing how learning happens in both a positive or negative way; my hair stylist's response was, *"Whenever you learn, it's always positive."*

* * * * *

I remember a class where we were learning the meaning of karma. Some felt karma reflected the lessons we have come to Earth to learn and heal during each incarnation and some believed that it is nonsense. The teacher asked all of us what we would do if we were walking down a street and witnessed a mother abusing her child. Would we keep walking, call for help, or intervene and tell

the mother to stop? Some said they would keep walking, because
what was going on with this family was solely between them and
their karma, as they believed we chose our parents for our lessons.
Others said they would intervene because they felt that destiny
placed them in their path for the intervention to take place as part
of a group karmic lesson. This is the one I chose.

* * * * *

One day, while I was working at a fair in Vancouver, British
Columbia, I heard one of my Universal Guides say, "It's time to
throw out the garbage, right now!" Without thinking, I walked
across the road and dropped my *half-filled* plastic bag into the
garbage receptacle. Halfway back to the tent, I was stopped in my
tracks when I overheard a phrase between a father and two pre-
school boys. One of the boys must have asked his father a question
which precipitated a familiar button-pushing phrase that my father
used, *"Because I said so!"*

After hearing those words, I walked over to the man and asked
him, "Are you a Cancer?"

"How did you know, are you psychic?" He answered.

"Yes," I responded. "But that's not why I asked you." I explained that my father always answered my questions with 'because I said so' whenever he chose not to answer me right away,
and he was a Cancer. I often wondered if putting off answering
immediately was a Cancer trait, although I'm sure it is used by
other signs as well. Hearing that phrase proved that those words
still had some power over me and it is quite possible that in the
future it could have the same impact on his children and their
attitude towards him.

I ended with, "Please take the time to answer when your children first ask you a question, since these are the formative years in
a child's life."

"What do you know? Are you also a parental counselor?" He
responded with irritation.

"Yes, among other things." I answered.

"Well our family is doing just fine the way it is, so mind your
own business!" He retorted.

His two sons looked at me with sad faces, a look I truly understood, as the father grabbed their hands and dragged them into the crowd.

"Denial is a veil to the conscious mind."

Since I was brought within earshot of this father's words and actions, I was given permission to intervene as part of their karma; solely on the children's behalf. Our meeting provided an exceptional learning experience that helped me to see that I had not fully resolved that issue with my father. Maybe it was Dad that called out about the garbage, which is quite humorous because Mom could never get him to take it out — I had to.

This karmic connection assisted me in releasing the "negative energy residue" I was still harboring or I would never have been asked to participate in yet another Universal set-up!

Unresolved Experiences

"Unresolved experiences are situations in your life which you are unable to cope with."

Some of my memories depict issues that I have held on to, deep within my subconscious and unknowingly remained as defeating baggage until I understood the who, why, when, and where that surrounded all my "original core issues." It was only then that I began to comprehend past unpleasant experiences and what they represented on a mental, physical and spiritual level. Bringing that knowledge to the surface, permitted me to release all that was keeping me from moving on.

Adverse feelings can cause dislike when working with that subject

My intense unfavorable association with numbers caused me to have difficulty with math that began when I was three, when Mom decided to teach me how to write numbers. I distinctly remember her disappointed look especially when she taught me how to write the number 8. I had trouble drawing the circles as round as she wanted them to be. All I knew was that I drew an eight the best I could. I believe this incident was *the original trauma for my problems with math.* Mom's look was similar to the disappointing glare I received from a math teacher years later.

In fifth grade, I had a math teacher in her late sixties that became easily impatient with her students whenever they failed to come up with the correct answers. One day she called me up to the board. As I approached the slate colored board covered in math problems, I could feel butterflies starting to rise in my stomach, working upward toward my throat and racing to my face. By the time I reached the board, I knew I would not know the answer. Seconds felt like hours as I stood facing the board. I heard footsteps coming towards me. I turned to see the teacher's hard, wrinkled face, as she stared at me. Within an instant, she slapped me. I turned, and with head bent low, shuffled back to my seat. I sobbed in shame and thought how could she be so cruel to embarrass me in front of my classmates, when my only crime was being scared and not understanding the problem.

It was only after seeing the whole picture while in therapy as an adult, did I understand I was holding onto my anger toward that teacher because *I was more hurt by appearing stupid in front of all my peers than the slap itself.*

When I understood the reason for all my anger toward her, the truth of what I felt that day was clear. I believe the teacher's anger might have come from her own feelings of not being able to reach me. I do not think anger or any other attitude is an excuse for slapping children.

To my dismay, my fear of numbers did not stop in school. It continued to crop up throughout my life such as when my father asked me to help him at his grocery store. Sometimes, when I worked the cash register, Dad would stand behind me and watch as I counted out the customer's change. I was already feeling the pressure of possibly giving out incorrect change without Dad adding to the situation. Most of the time, as fear clogged my judgment, mistakes happened.

"When an uncomfortable incident is not 'nipped in the bud,' it skyrockets into a continuous fear throughout your life."

A child may react negatively toward any subject when it is not taught in a loving and patient manner. To this day I still feel uneasy when working with numbers, so, I surrender to any uneasy feelings and use a calculator. If I make a mistake, so be it.

* * * * *

When I was 10, my parents sent me to a Girl Scout Camp in New Jersey. At camp, all the girls showered together in one large bathing facility. I felt self-conscious about anyone seeing my body, because in my household you had to be completely clothed. If I was partially clothed, I could tell it embarrassed my parents, most likely because of their strict upbringing. I found it difficult to bathe with the other girls, and I did not understand why. I would seek out periods when no one was around to take a shower alone or have a sponge bath. One day, after walking into my assigned bungalow, I was attacked by a group of girls wielding hairbrushes. They thought I refused to bathe with them because I was stuck-up and too good for them. (The same assumption was parroted by others throughout my school years.) My attackers were unaware that my actions had nothing to do with them but the circumstances in which I was raised.

I discovered I had inadvertently taken on my parent's issues of propriety. To help me overcome my shyness, I became a Go-Go dancer wearing a sequined costume. Later on, I really took it off when I became an artist's model.

* * * * *

I created a life of stuffing my emotions, which most likely caused my respiratory allergies and poor digestion. (There were a lot of things I could not stomach)

I found it difficult to relate to or show any feelings when I was 16 with John, my boyfriend at the time. John often told me that he loved me, but I was incapable of returning those feelings. Those three 'not so little' words were missing from my families vocabulary and not demonstrated enough to bring about a positive effect. How could I recognize an emotion so foreign to me? This learned behavior played a big part in my break-up with John, who to this day, has been the only love of my life. If I had married John or anyone at the start of my metaphysical career, I would not be doing the work I love. Remember, *everything happens in Divine order.*

When I turned 17 and got my driver's license, I felt free to come and go for the first time in my life. The world was my oyster, I could let down my hair, throw caution to the wind and live my life to the fullest, *the way I wanted*. I found a wonderful bar in Manhattan where, thanks to Mom for teaching me to dance, I became "Miss Popularity" and danced until all hours of the night. The barflies became my surrogate family and through their acceptance and kindness, I learned to recognize and express love. With their help I was finally able to love myself and respond in kind to others.

"Unless you change a negative situation into a positive, it will remain a negative"

* * * * *

I discovered one day that I was funny. Learning how to diffuse anger with laughter within my household and school became second nature to me. I was so good that I got tagged a wise-guy and often ended up in detention hall. When people laughed at my shenanigans; *they were paying attention to me.* The downside was everything became a joke. When I was laughing I was not crying, something I did a lot in my youth. Looking back at all the subterfuge I used in order to be heard and loved saddens me.

I remember when I attended lectures how boring most of the teachers were, hence the reason I teach with a sense of humor. When the people are laughing, I know they are awake and having fun. Therefore, I believe that *"A sense of humor makes good sense."* Although I enjoyed being funny I felt uncomfortable standing alone in front of an audience. Upon asking for guidance, I was reminded of a situation when I had an uncomfortable experience of being laughed at while alone on stage.

I was the Master of Ceremony of my high school play. After my first monologue, I was to spin around, model-style, and exit through the center of a dark burgundy velvet curtain after it opened. My monologue went smoothly but after I made my perfect pivot, there was no parting of the way. I desperately clawed at the curtain while the auditorium roared with laughter. I searched in vain for the illusive opening that would lead me out of my predicament. Finally, I located it, and escaped.

Thirty years later, I trusted that the effects of this one embarrassing moment passed into oblivion; there had not been any repeats when I appeared in plays, improvisational comedy or during speaking engagements, but then again, I was not alone on stage. Once, I was asked to compete in a stand-up comedy contest at Tranquillity Park in downtown Houston. I felt confident enough to accept the challenge, however, the more I rehearsed, the more intolerable the whole situation became; I decided with a sigh of relief, to cancel my appearance.

A few years later an opportunity arrived to overcome my fear when I was asked to go up on stage, by myself, to talk about the healing properties of crystals. Crystals are a passion with me; something I really enjoy talking about. All went well towards turning my past negative experience into a positive and productive one. I was comforted by a room filled with my metaphysical loving peers and a guidance system I have come to trust. Feeling their love radiating out helped me leap past my fear of speaking alone. Now, talking on stage about what I love comes easy with 'a little help from my friends' and my Celestial Guides.

All this remembering explained the core of my fears and how, "When I let go of the past I am free to move on."

"Know that we are never alone when we ask for help from our Universal Guides and the teachers that surround us."

Living experiences are one way, but understanding them is paramount. Uncovering hidden meanings and innuendoes remaining as negative reminders of a past long forgotten in your subconscious. Surfing the subconscious is the only way to find the imprinted messages *that must be resolved* so you may reclaim the 'you' that is *the original "Child of God."*

CHAPTER 2

Be All You Can Be!

It is time to get on with your life!

A point of Universal Fact: *"We were born Whole without the* **need** *for anyone in our life* **to be whole.***"* One of our most important missions in life is to find out *who we really are.*

If we chose not to claim our independence, we remain the sum total of our parents and *all* who enter our life, with all their behavior patterns and personality traits both positive and negative, including all desperate and unfulfilled relationships, as you blindly search for love and approval. If the limited beliefs of our parents and relationships did not allow them to become all they can be, it will not aid us.

We come into this life as a perfect creation. Somewhere along life's path, doubts and feelings of inadequacies develop from what we learned growing up; contributing to loss of our Divine perfection or stimulating the "I am unworthy" syndrome. When these feelings are in full swing, we start to believe, in order to feel good about ourselves, that *we need someone outside ourselves in order to accomplish the feeling of being complete.*

When you feel complete and happy and in your power, you will then bring in a partner to *share in your Wholeness,* your Dharmic partner, your soul-purpose-partner and someone you will not want or feel the need to change. Someone who will not want to, change, bully or control you into feeling you are nothing without them. *Remember, no one can do anything to you without your permission.*

Living in solitude can be a great way towards finding a healthier you and helps to re-connect us with The Universal Wisdom. Some of my clients misconstrue this suggestion as hiding, and claim it leads to loneliness and/or depression. I explained that when one feels a deep connection to Spirit, loneliness never enters the perfect picture. Depression is a healthy form of going deep within when searching for answers, and is beneficial as long as you emerge quickly and in touch with what was bothering you. Spending delighted time with your true Higher Self, Guides and teachers is beneficial and quite rewarding.

Learning to understand and embrace yourself with all your idiosyncrasies is the first step to discovering that your Wholeness is foremost, especially when you begin to recognize how and why you bring the partners into your life where you place them first — over and above your own happiness and peace of mind.

When a client feels they are no one without their other half I ask "Who are these *other halves* you say you are endlessly searching for and continue to believe will *make you feel happy?*" I have a profound message for you, "There is no other half that can make you feel whole — **you are already whole.** This healthier form of thinking allows you to release the misperception that you are only half a person without that someone in our life."

"I am one, you are one, but we can be one together!"

A constant diet of unwholesome encounters tends to close our heart and we start to feel that we will never find that special someone. When I followed this limited road, I placed my work on the back burner. Now, I put my energy into my work, which is a perfect relationship unto itself, and *when I am ready,* a truly happy unique relationship that is a compliment to both of us, will be known to me.

"Give yourself time to release that which keeps you from being and staying in your most powerful state of consciousness."

When you feel *Whole,* and are fully in touch with your understanding of your mission on Earth, you will be ready to welcome in a partner that truly compliments your Wholeness.

"You are a perfect Child of God destined to do great things."

Bringing in your Dharmic (on-purpose) career

In order to find a job that will be your life's work and bring you the happiness you deserve, you must stop jumping from one unfulfilling work experience to another, believing the next job will be better. We chose to act this way instead of putting in the effort of working on ourselves towards creating that perfect career.

Arlene, a native Texan, came to me because she did not wish to continue with her chosen profession as an attorney. She said she decided on this particular career because she thought she could make a difference in the judiciary system. After being in the legal field for many years, she realized her beliefs were unrealistic. She said she now understood the slogan, "You can't fight City Hall." All Arlene accomplished was to make herself emotionally and physically ill. She began to use food as a substitute for the gratification she was not getting from her job or her uneventful life. This led to obesity. I asked her if she no longer wanted to work in the legal arena, where she did want to work? She said, "More than anything, I want to teach school." A year ago she left her job, went to Santa Fe and found a job teaching Native American children in a small nonprofit school. She received a pittance, compared to her fees as an attorney, but it included room and board; at the time it was all she needed. She recognized that teaching children was her true calling. The only reason she came back to Texas was because of family and money problems. She made several attempts to locate a teaching position in Texas, but was told she did not have enough experience. *Here is a perfect example of what can happen when we are forced to leave a dream job because of lack of money as many of my Lightworking associates say they had done.*

Arlene remained in Texas and once again she took a job with a law firm. She came to me when her life had became intolerable and did not know what to do. After our session she had the courage to fly to Washington state, where several schools were searching for teachers. When she returned, she told me she felt that one of the schools was impressed with her, and there was a possibility she would be hired. After what we discussed during our session clicked, Arlene was ready to once again catch up with her dream. She was offered the job and would be leaving in six months for Olympia.

There was an extra Universal bonus to this story. Arlene belonged to Overeaters Anonymous and decided to call a male sponsor whom she never met face to face, but enjoyed talking with. She told him she was leaving soon and asked him if he wanted to meet. They made arrangements to meet at an OA meeting. She told me that the moment she looked into George's "baby browns," she knew he was the man destined for her. A month later, I received an invitation to their wedding.

When Arlene realized that placing her needs first was more important than her altruistic need to change the world, she healed all that was keeping her stuck. This brought her a happier life with her Dharmic partner and a new career. George gave up his job in Texas and they moved to Washington together. This miracle took place within three months of our first and only visit.

When you allow your healing to take place, you are free and open to bring in a partner and career for your Highest Good.

How The Universe works through me

When I begin working with someone, invariably, the first question a woman usually asks is, "Can you help me find a man?" The man will ask, "Can you help me find a better job so I can make more money?" I always answer with "No, but I'll help you find yourself." I explain that when they are finally ready to stop bringing in all their unfulfilling relationships I can help them. I will provide the tools and information that will assist them in understanding why they emotionally let their obsessive patterns rule them. By clearly knowing how, why and when they became this unhappy and unproductive person, they are closer towards finding peace and contentment. Once all is understood, they will no longer be dependent on me or anyone else for answers and this emotional pumping up, will in turn, help them prepare for the partner and job they have been searching for.

"When you stop searching and place that energy into healing the past, all will manifest in Divine Order."

Feelings of abandonment, low self worth, limitations and emotional demons will resurface no matter who you bring into your life for that quick-fix relationship. Unless the underlying causes of the original pattern addictions are brought to the attention of the conscious mind and released, you are not emotionally equipped to open your heart, mind and body.

Be true to numero uno

The best way to heal *number one* is to be true to yourself. People will have more respect for you when you assert this. I have had clients tell me that their husband did not respect them or understand their needs. I tell them that if this is what they are feeling, it is because they do not respect or understand themselves. Other people can feel when you have poor self-worth. When they disrespect you, they are only returning what you are mirroring to them. In other words if you want to feel something, whether it be respect, happiness or love, first give it to yourself. When speaking to the husbands, they tell me they are glad when their wives finally stood up to their abuse. They tell me that the only way they could get their attention was to yell or hit them; it was hurting them to have to constantly act out in this way. This form of sadomasochistic behavior usually occurs when a person grows up in an abusive environment and it becomes their way of life. The best way to diffuse an out-of-control situation is *just say no* to the abuser.

Our mind can also be relentless and extremely abusive when it wants to get our attention. One way is by playing our negative 'trauma drama tapes' to excess. When you earnestly tell your mind, *stop* or *no*, it must instantly change its obsessive verbal abuse and listen to your command. When you are back in control, go over each thought; make sense of them. When you give yourself permission to hear the tapes being played like a broken record in your mind, this will transmute *all unwanted negative* thoughts into productive positive ones.

"Now when I open my heart, I only bring in those for my Highest Good and soul growth."

Another way in which we tend to fill the voids in our life is with food. This temporary high or escape from what is really bothering you can only serve to lead to what I call the "open-mouth-insert-food syndrome." We may not have complete control over our life, but we certainly have control over what we put in our mouth. People who have a chronic empty feeling in their life know that eating their troubles does not work and only leads to obesity. Growing up, most of us were comforted with the use of food, such as when we cried. Some mothers who chose to believe we were crying only because we were hungry would find something to stick in our mouths to quiet us. Sometimes food was used as a bribe; telling us we could have dessert only when we cleaned our plate and we did, like good human vacuum cleaners. And the ever popular guilt trip; eat all your food, think of all the poor starving children in the world.

My attitude with food was quite unique. Dad owned a grocery store, so there was no lack of food as there was a lack of verbal love. But since I wanted his love, *as usual,* food became a substitute for that love. I wanted him to hug me and show me how much he loved me. This association with food became a *sore spot* in my stomach and I developed chronic indigestion problems, eventually leading to the removal of my gall bladder.

Add these addiction to the all consuming need to please others and what a wild merry-go-round our life becomes! Even after pointing out that the need to take care of and help others above their own needs is considered an addiction, some clients will hold their addictive ground and say that they *enjoy* helping others just to see them smile. They tell me they do not want to stop helping others because it reassures them that they are loved. Some say they do not see anything wrong with making people happy. When I ask them when is it their turn to receive as good as they give, they respond with, "Helping others *is* as good as it gets. If it doesn't hurt them, I don't understand why I should stop!" I explain that when you consistently give attention to others, over and above yourself, you tend to ignore your own needs. This pattern keeps you from getting in touch with, and releasing your own inner difficulties and obstacles, also known as denial. That usually gets them thinking, but only when they are ready to understand how their actions are affecting their life.

Some people will do anything to be liked. This can become down right exhausting to those who are the recipients of their compulsions. The hospitable ones who are receiving, learn how to deal with a pleasers obsessions after they understand that their action comes second nature to them. The pleaser acts this way in order to feel much needed outside love and acceptance. These actions become out of control, due to their 'poor-me feelings' of being unloved in their childhood. The recipients, unfortunately, do not have the heart to stop them. They, too, are acting out their own addiction of not hurting others, even if they are feeling overwhelmed.

"Addiction is a two way street; a give and take, or the 'blind addict leading the blind."

During a class, a facilitator asked, "What is your purpose on the planet?" I responded, "I want to heal the planet and as many people as I can." "Stop!" She said. "That is not what you were brought here to do. You must *first work on yourself.* If everyone worked on themselves there would be no need for anyone to heal anybody and we can live in a wonderful world filled with physically, mentally and spiritually awakened beings."

An example I use to describe how important it is for you take care of yourself first, is when you are on a plane and the flight attendant says, "After your oxygen mask falls down in front of you, *first* place the mask on yourself, then your children."

What good is the mask on the child if you are unconscious and unable to help them?

The Mirror Image Technique and its effects

This technique helps you to get in touch with your "I Am," leading towards empowerment and connecting to your Higher Self. Also, with the use of a mirror, it permits you to see beyond your pain and the underlying causes of problems with those you want to make amends with.

One way of using the mirror effect to release the past is to ask yourself what you specifically dislike about a person. Go within and you will see what you dislike about them is what you dislike about yourself. When those in your life are mirroring an emotion back to you, such as anger, it shows that you have not completely healed whatever the issue represents to you. Another exercise is to ask what you like about that person, and by doing this you will find what you like about yourself.

When you ask these questions of all the people you have been with in the past and those that are still a part of your life, you may uncover some interesting facts towards understanding the true reasons that are keeping you from moving forward.

"It doesn't matter if you don't understand the cause of your distress, just be willing to let it go."

When you let go, nothing will annoy you and you will continue in peace without the anger that might have taken over your calm when an irritating situation is mirrored to you — similar to the buttons that get pushed.

"No one or anything can incite you unless there are unresolved issues attached to an unhappy memory or action."

The final exercise is to look into your own eyes while standing in front of a mirror. Allow yourself to feel your parents within and say, "I am not my mother. I am not my father." This is especially helpful when you unknowingly repeat their phrases or act out emotions that you have seen or heard your parents do, even after you swore you would never do it. Like most of us, you probably have found that hard to live up to. This is normal because they were our first teachers until we left and went out on our own. If the negative actions you have inadvertently copied did not work for your parents, such as lack of prosperity, abundance, happiness, healthy relationship, and peace of mind, they will not work for you. Parents are your role models until you let them go and become the adult you want to be.

"When you are tired of being part of the school of hard-knocks join the school of "God-knocks," and all will be open to you."

If you chose to no longer act out patterns or childhood negative memories, then look into the mirror and find the true, happy, carefree, healthy adult staring back at you that you can live with. Say to your powerful mirror image, the true you, "I Am... " and proudly say your name. Learn to see yourself as perfect, whole and complete. When you look in the mirror see yourself as, "*Perfection in, perfection out*" and others will acknowledge your perfection.

No matter how many times you are told how beautiful or wonderful you are, unless you allow *yourself* to feel those words, you will not know how to accept a compliment. The inner child was hurt so long ago may refuse to let go of its pain, trauma or anguish; it is used to fighting for what it wants. Therefore, it is up to you, as the adult, to communicate unconditional love to it. Give your inner child the love, attention (or whatever) it never received in order to heal the past issues. If you find yourself saying or doing something you regret or have no idea why it is happening, you can bet it is your scared inner child, not the adult, acting out. You and your inner child must be loved back into the fold for you to have any chance of becoming whole.

> *"It does not matter why other people act out;*
> *it's how you react that is important."*

Touching the Lion on the Nose

Touching the Lion on the Nose is a meditative exercise I use in my practice when clients tell me they are ready to end an unhappy and sometimes debilitating connection with the past. This method helps release negative feelings when emotionally tied to others and left unresolved from childhood and past lives, in a quick and easy way. I start by guiding them into a meditation that brings them quickly into a Theta state, deeper than Alpha or the space just before sleep. The mind does not physically need to "face" those you have issues with in order to resolve them; you will visually bring in those you wish to confront but were unable to on a physical level for whatever reason. You will then be able to safely face your lions and tell them with love, not judgment, how you really feel about the unhappy relationship. The Universe will direct your message to all concerned with Love and Light.

*   *   *   *   *

A frightened woman walked into my store one day and told me a story about her husband. In a fit of rage, he killed both of their children and threatened to kill her the next time he saw her. Even through prison walls, his threat and the memory of her children's murder had an emotional hold on her, keeping her trapped in fear. The plot definitely sounded like a made-for-TV special! All she could say was that she hated him. I told her what she was feeling was understandable, but her husband probably had lived around hate all his life.

I explained to her that I had a theory that those who act out to such a degree, where their actions lead to murder, are incapable of loving themselves or anyone. Somewhere in their lives, murderers chose not to recognize the difference between right and wrong, a moral code that would let one know that killing is vile and improper behavior, "thou shall not kill." This code is best described by Menander in one of his works from the book *Monostikoi*, which states, "Conscious is a God to all mortals." This extreme acting out behavior possibly stems from living in an environment surrounded by hatred. This hatred most likely came from feelings of, "no one loves me" or "I am unlovable." After she completed her story, I went on to explain that her husband is still feeling powerful emotions of hate and hostility, perpetuated to even a higher degree by his incarceration and that he needs to feel something more than a constant diet of hate, in order for him to be able to reprogram this thinking and his behavior.

I suggested that I guide her through the "Touching the Lion on the Nose" meditation. She agreed, so, I asked her to close her eyes and imagine her and her husband facing each other; she sitting in one chair and her husband in the other. I told her to look into his eyes and instead of adult eyes filled with anger and rage, see the eyes of the inner child that had acted out in pain.

"It is the unhappy inner child that lashes out in confusion from an unresolved past."

Next, I whispered to her to tell him with love and understanding, and not judgment, all she ever wanted to tell him but was too afraid to. The type of relationship she would have liked to have had with him, how she felt about the death of their two children and his threats to kill her; including any incident that had to do with family members. When she finished talking with him, I guided her to see both of them stand up and watch him walk away. Then I told her to first surround herself with the 'Pink Light of Unconditional Love' sending a stream out to him, from the center of her heart between the breastbone, while saying, *"I now give all up to the Holy Spirit to transmute, forgive and forget. So be it. Praise God."*

When she was finished, I told her that The Universe would direct the releasing, empowered conversation she had with her husband, and when she thought of him, she was to continue directing this 'Pink Light' out to him instead of hate. By continually using this 'Healing Light of Love' as therapy for herself and her husband, a transformation will take place for all concerned.

When we finished the session on her husband, she confided in me that she also had an abusive father. I now understood why she was consistently attracting men who also abused her. This pattern continued because she was continually searching for a way to get love from her father; in her mind all men acted like her father.

My client called me about a week later and told me that she definitely felt less anger toward her husband, all because I helped her to understand that it was possible that unresolved issues from a person's past could create an out-of-control violent behavior, as demonstrated by her husband. When this brave lady chose to stop feeding the energy that stoked the fire of his hatred and fears, she was ready to live a more fulfilling life; free from fear and pain and with hope in her heart for the future.

"To conquer others is to have power; to conquer yourself is to know"

I have read about incidents where prisoners were completely changed for the good when they allowed God's love back into their lives. It released the negative energy that bound them to darkness throughout their incarceration and even after their release into society. This miracle is known as "Finding God."

"Replacing hate and fear with Love and Light has changed many an incarcerated being."

* * * * *

Another time I used "Touching the Lion on the Nose" was after a woman phoned me and said she felt as if she had been summoned to take care of some unfinished business with her ex-husband and his parents; all of whom she could not tolerate. She told me that the whole time she was married she only felt anger and blatant rejection from the in-laws, which led to resentment on both sides. I invited her to come to my home that evening to teach her how to send Love and Light instead of her usual dislike to the ex's living in Texas. When she arrived, I guided her through the meditation, releasing those pent-up emotions. When she finished, she purchased a Rose Quartz egg that I suggested she take with her on the two hour drive to face her lions-in-law. I suggested the pink crystal because it represents unconditional love for yourself and those around you.

I explained to her that during the trip, whenever she thought of her ex-husband and his family, she was to hold the egg next to her heart to accentuate the stream of "Pink Light Love Energy" she was sending out to all concerned. Reaching out to anyone in this manner, helps to transmute feelings of anger. When she arrived, she was to surround herself, then the house, with the "Pink Light." She telephoned me the next day and said, in a relieved voice, that while she was walking up to their door she took a deep breath and sent the Light around herself and the house as I suggested. After she knocked, the door opened and she was both shocked and amazed to see the whole family *smiling*. When she walked in, they all hugged her! It was all so unexpected and they shared the best quality time ever. She ended with, "This love transmuting the anger stuff really works!"

Whenever you are feeling emotions other than Love, surround yourself with the "Pink Light of Unconditional Love." This Light represents all that is Heavenly and will transmute all negative feelings and actions into a pure Love state. By sending out Love and Light from your aura (the electromagnetic energy field that surrounds your body, up to 25 ft.) will always be received with love.

"When love meets love and heart meets heart, love is all there is."

My client found out by changing her feelings and opening her heart to Love, her in-laws responded in kind. If you know someone likes or dislikes you, it is human nature to return the same feelings. Remember, *it is important to release all negative energy that surrounds you from a past you are not at peace with*. Had she decided not to deal with the animosity permeating her being, she would have continued seething whenever she thought of her in-laws. It is best to face your lions and get on with your life in order to live in peace and harmony.

"Unburdening hate, the opposite of love, and replacing it with Love and Light does not take long, because love moves mountains and changes all mistrust, hostilities and fear."

* * * * *

While I was teaching at a fair in Vancouver, a woman came into my tent and said she was in need of guidance about a man she had met only two weeks before. She told me she felt an unusual attrac-tion for him, both mentally and physically, but she did not know if he felt the same way. This man lived in Vancouver, but was moving to Australia within a week. It seems that he enjoyed Australia so much while on vacation a few weeks prior, that he decided to live there. She told me she was afraid to tell him how she felt for fear he may not want to see her during his remaining time in Vancouver.

"The power of love surpasses all in a time of indecision."

I told her I would guide her through an exercise called Touch-ing the Lion on the Nose where she could talk with him in a medi-tative state and tell him what she was feeling. She said she was not sure if she could put into words what she was feeling. I asked her if she wanted to know before he left, if his feelings were mutual or if he was only taking advantage of the situation. There was also the possibility that he also felt the same way as she, but too afraid to tell her. Upon hearing this, she happily agreed. While in Theta, she visualized him walking in and sitting in the chair opposite her. When she was finished, she told me that she felt as if a tremendous weight had been lifted from her shoulders and her heart felt lighter.

I shared with her that while she was in Theta, I received a strong message that there was another reason for her love-at-first-sight meet-ing with this irresistible man. It seems it was time for them to meet and once again live in Australia, a country where they both loved each other in another incarnation. *Sounds like the makings of a great Meryl Streep movie; only I would call it "Out Of Australia!"*

As she was walking away, I called out to her, "I sure wish I was going to Australia." She quickly turned her head back and said,

"So do I!" I answered, "I believe you've made your decision." She gave me a smile that let me know all would be well and kept walking. I felt the familiar chill bumps that I get when I know what has transpired is Universal truth.

Chill bumps are The Universal goose-bumps that appear on your arms or throughout your entire body, confirming that what was just said, heard or seen contains the truth.

✶ ✶ ✶ ✶ ✶

At the same fair, I was teaching Astrology and Numerology by imputing the birth dates of customers into the computer and printing out pertinent data concerning their behavior patterns. After going through the first 100 charts, I started to see in over half, an unproductive behavior pattern clearly emerging. Continuing with the interpretative interviews with over a thousand participants in 17 days, I found that over 50% read high caution tendencies. I intuitively asked the participants if they had a fear of the future. They all said yes. The initial fear caused them to be stuck in indecision. Most of those I interviewed were not doing what they wanted or happy in general, whether in a job or relationship. I told them it was their chronic indecision that was keeping them stuck. I also told them, heal the past and live in the now. Since you cannot do anything about what you cannot see, feel, or touch in the future, why put energy into a time that does not exist yet? Whatever you accomplish or change in the now, becomes your future.

"Stay in the now and live your Divine life to the fullest."

I asked guidance what would cause such an unproductive pattern. My Guides' answered, "High caution will affect decisions pertaining to people's future, creating procrastination stemming from a constant flow of negative childhood conditioning." They also told me, that most parents tend to begin conversations with their children with *be careful, you'd better not, make sure you don't, don't talk to strangers, watch out for your sister/brother, make sure you come right home after school, you'd better call me if you are going to be late* or *be careful crossing the street*. These are valid instructions that may keep your child safe. But starting any sentence with a negative command, such as "don't," tends to accomplish the

opposite of your goal. Also, using negatives as a method of rein-
forcement will only instill unnecessary fear in the child. Most children have learned to tune out negative words, all they hear is *forget*
and *they most likely will.* As in, "Don't *forget* to come right home
after school.

There are also phrases that do nothing to encourage self-esteem, such as, *You are always in my way, You never do anything
right, You are never around when I need you, You never listen to me,*
or *You are stupid (or dumb).* I met a man who thought his name
was "Dummy" until he entered kindergarten. Starting a sentence
with 'you' sounds accusatory and is tantamount to a slap in the
face when included with negatives or shouting.

Problems occur when a child does not follow your direction or
any one who may have their best interest at heart. Things like, if a
child stayed out past their curfew, and something horrible happens
like a molestation or being hit by a car. Or if something happens to
a sibling while in an older child's care. If the parent expresses, "It's
all your fault because you don't (or never) listen to what you are
told." Growing up, the child only remembers fear and guilt associ-
ated with the memory that, *something bad will happen when they do
not listen* to a spouse, employer or any authoritative person. After
they do anything that seems wrong or remotely similar to the original issue, the feelings, indelibly imprinted and hidden from the
subconscious mind, will return as an instant deja vu. As an adult,
past negative memories will return as extreme caution when a decision has to be made, and will prevail when dealing with any situation that makes them uncomfortable. With caution factor high; it
leads to indecision and procrastination, and later on down the road,
victimization from authoritative out of control addicts!

Learn to start sentences to your children, or anyone for that
matter, with positives and reinforcements such as, *remember to come
straight home from school so you can have more time to play before
dinner.* This will give them a reason to remember *not* to forget. If
you wish to connect with your children in a more loving and spiritual way, sit down with them and introduce the why, when and
where of things which will accomplish more than just the "don'ts."
Instill *love and safety* not *fear.*

*"Whenever you think you are controlling a situation you are
really out of control."*

This is an incident from my childhood when my mother gave me
an opposing message by using the word 'don't' at the beginning of
her sentence. Before eating, Mom would say, "Don't let your clothes
eat too," therefore, whenever I ate, I became so nervous not to spill
my food that I did just that. This imprint still remains with me and
has ruined many an expensive piece of apparel.

One evening, I was dining at a restaurant when I overheard a
young mother say Mom's phrase to her child. I walked over to her
and told her that my Mother used to say the same thing to me and
it never stopped me from spilling my food. The more careful I
was, the more nervous I became and this fear even kept me from
enjoying and digesting my food. I asked her if there was a possibility that the next time she gave her child food she could simply say,
"enjoy it." She smiled at me and I felt her silent thanks.

Going outside The Universal Realm for your answers

This section is for those who feel they must *continually* seek out
counselors, therapists, and healers. I also include those who attend
conferences, lectures, symposiums and classes. Those of you, you know
who you are, do not use what you have learned to get on with your
own life. You still have not grasped that going within and working
with your Higher Self is the best way to tap into the never-ending
resources toward peace of mind or the highest form of contentment
— bliss. All avenues are open to you within The Universal Realm;
your Guides, Angels, and all there is — when you ask.

When you attend classes or seminars, you are searching outside your Higher Self or your Universal Guides and will learn what
these facilitators believe. By going within, you will learn *the truth
that is right for you*. That is why at my classes I start with, "Come,
listen to what I don't know. Take what you need and feels good in
your heart and leave the rest." The more I listen to myself say the
things I need to know, the more I practice what I teach. This is
one of the reasons for writing this book — sometimes even I get
tired of listening to my own voice.

I truly understand this need to attend classes and seminars, because I too have bopped from doctor to hospital, chiropractor to nutritionist, psychologist to psychiatrist in a vain attempt to receive some form of attention, I desperately felt was missing in my life, whether it be a gentle voice, a soft touch or quick-fix, also known as the 'Band-Aid effect.' I used this behavior pattern as a survival mode just to feel alive, especially when I asked myself, *"Who am I?"* and *"Where am I going?"*

The following eye opening words are from a song on Barbra Streisand's 1966 album "Color Me Barbra," written by D. Fields and C. Coleman which I listened to quite often in my late teens. These lyrics certainly described my conundrum during the free love, drug era of the 1960's.

Where Am I Going?
Where am I going and what will I find?
What's in this grab bag that I call, my mind?
What am I doing alone on a shelf,
Ain't it a shame, but no one's to blame but myself
When you lost your way year after year.
Do I keep falling in love for just the kick of it?
Stammering through the thin and thick of it
hating each old tired trick of it
Know what I am? I'm good and sick of it!
Run where it's foul, run where it's fair
No matter where I run, I meet myself there.
Looking inside me, what do I see?
Anger, hope and doubt,
what am I all about and where am I going?

Stammering through life, year after year, is where I found myself. Could this be where you find yourself? If you are always going outside yourself for your answers, when will you find the time to put what you have learned from others into practice? If you believe that by being in the presence and energy of 'Lightworking sharers of wisdom' is the way to make everything better without any work on your part, I have a wake-up call for you; *it doesn't work that way!* I spent a small fortune doing all this 'going outside for help stuff' until one day I came to the conclusion that "there had to be a better way!" That was the day I began to go within and listen to my inner voice and Guides for *my true answers.*

"Go within and find comfort from life's daily escalators."

Tuning In

I was trained in a former life on how to dispense Reiki energy, an ancient form of Chinese hands-on healing. In order to use the Reiki name on my business card, I was told by a Reiki Master that I would first have to take a class and receive a certificate. So, I decided to invest the money and take the class. There are three levels and after each level is completed, you go through a secret meditative induction. During my induction, I saw a Chinese boy I knew was me in a past life. With me was my Reiki Master, a sacred looking man wearing a long white robe and a beard to match. I was so happy to once again be with him. I gazed into my Master's eyes and asked, "Master, when will I know peace?" (It felt as if I was playing Grasshopper in the TV show *Kung Fu.*) His answer was, *"When one goes within, one is never without."*

The times when I feel scattered and unbalanced and believe that I am not getting clear advice from within, I tend to revert back to the old ways of seeking outside assistance from psychics or others. Usually what they tell me I have already heard from my Guides. When I fall back into these old patterns, The Universe will pop in and *bellow,* (almost like the Wizard of Oz!) "Are you ready to listen to the all knowing Higher intelligence within you?" To which I answer, with a sigh of relief, "I'm ready. Open me to the truth. Show me the way. Guide me on the easy and effortless path!" Remember the parable about having "faith the size of a mustard seed?" When we have faith in ourselves and re-connect with the holy intention, focus, balance and the Guides that are here to help us, we are as powerful as The Earth's Universal energy. I also remember that the old ways of seeking my answers always sabotages what would have resulted in a speedier and more peaceful outcome if I had only checked in with Universal Wisdom in the first place.

"Surround yourself with those on the path of enlightenment."

Making your Soul connections

Many souls are brought together intuitively. When someone's energy field is compatible with yours, you are spiritually tuned in. These physical energy fields will locate the souls that manifest a safe familiarity to you. When you are open, you recognize them among the Lightworkers who come to you in your desire to be all you can be. When you take the time to find and open to your particular soul partners in this incarnation, your emotional and physical healing is swift.

"When one is ready to release any harmful tendencies,
the recovery is swift and painless."

One year, I placed an ad in the Unity Church Directory to advertise my unique field of intuitive spiritual counseling. Several weeks later I received a call from a lady named Barbara. She told me that even though there were several other therapists in the directory, she felt guided to call me for an appointment. When she arrived, I greeted a woman standing about 4'7" with an obvious liver ailment (her eyes and skin were yellow). The emotion for the liver and gall bladder manifests itself in "being stuck." This condition usually occurs when one is unhappy with a job, relationship or life.

"Dis-ease is caused by emotions not fully realized."

Our talks uncovered that Barbara was displeased with her job but continued working there because she needed the money, thus creating a physical ailment that allowed her to take two weeks off, *with pay,* to get well. During the sessions, I made three suggestions to help her. The *first* was to leave the job. I explained to her that whatever was creating her problems would eventually show up at the next job, within a month or so, unless she understood the cause of the original emotional issues and healed them. I told her she needed to understand why these feelings were emerging when her co-workers pushed her buttons. I explained that the people she chose to blame for her unhappiness could be her greatest teachers; mirroring her core unresolved childhood issues.

The *second* suggestion was to look at her co-workers; really look. Barbara needed to see them as children of God; in pain or acting out in anger, possibly after having a fight with a loved one or uncomfortable words with another employee. Suddenly she was in front of them, receiving their misplaced anger. Remember, I told her, they also have their stuff to work out.

"It doesn't matter why people act as they do,
it's how you react to them that is important."

The *third* suggestion was she needed to change her own attitude. Barbara needed to change how she felt and reacted to what would be coming up during her adjustment period. After the verbal part of the consultation, I performed a Reiki healing session on her for three consecutive days. By the fourth day she was totally free of her visible physical ailment — surprising her medical doctor. Barbara was now ready to deal with the emotions that she would be facing when she returned to work.

I saw her at church six months later and asked her. "How is your life going? "Great!" She replied. I also asked her, "Did you quit your job?" She told me when she understood why she had created her liver-stuckness problem, everything else fell into place. Instead of leaving, she decided to remain at her job and learn what she needed before moving on. Barbara also declared how much happier she felt after facing her problems instead of running away from them, as she had done in the past.

"When you are ready, the teachers come or you will seek them out."

When she followed my advice about changing her attitude, the people around her changed and everything worked out in Divine Order. She also learned that when anger, hostility and negative thoughts are aimed towards another, or when negative energy is deposited into the air from our words or energy field, people will feel and reflect this negativity back on us. When one stays at an unhappy position for money or health benefits, physical unrest will ensue. The career you want is the one that, when you ask yourself, "Would I be willing to work even if I didn't get paid?" and you can honestly answer YES.

Work that is fun becomes your on purpose mission and one of the many reasons for coming back to Earth this life.

"It's OK to get paid for what you enjoy doing the most."

Remember the old adage, "To thine own self be true?" This phrase is talking about selflessness, not selfishness, as some were taught to believe.

"Selflessness is not selfishness; serve yourself first!"

Staying anywhere you are unhappy, leaves you unfulfilled and brings only misery, as physical ailments will commonly occur. Usually the money earned under these circumstances goes toward doctors and therapists bills, medicine, or even a visit to the hospital. This also applies when staying in a relationship solely out of fear that no one wants you because you believe that this situation is better than nothing. *If a situation is nothing to begin with, with no potential for improvement, then you are not losing anything by giving it up for something better.* It is a Catch-22 situation. What do you do? Remember, "when one door closes another one opens."

I looked forward to getting fired or quitting, so I could start a new adventure—each one better than the next.

Learn to appreciate yourself. Know that unless you create a vacuum by releasing that which is not for your Highest Good and soul growth, you will remain stuck in a life filled with resentment, disappointment and most likely take part in *painful accidents of faith* and lots of dis-ease.

Problems do not go away by jumping from relationship to relationship, job to job or even changing your environment. If you believe your problems are not your fault, and tend to blame everyone else instead of taking responsibility for your actions or reactions during stressful situations, I have a message for you:

"You are the problem and the captain of your fate!"

In any relationship, you bring your old baggage into the lives of others; it is useless to blame others for pushing the buttons that get your attention, because this in turn *helps* you to face a reality openly screaming, *"you have not healed the past!"*

CHAPTER 3

Divine Guidance

*"A coincidence is a miracle in which God wishes
to remain anonymous."* — Dr. Gerald Jampolski

We all grow up; first being guided by our parents, then school
teachers and friends. As adults, we often ask ourselves, *Why isn't
my life working out the way I want it to?* or *Why am I so unhappy?*
When you ask these questions, you are ready to embark on a path
of enlightenment that comes from your inner guidance, the Higher
Self, the outside Universal Realm of God, Jesus, and all that there
is. Open to others who wish to help too, such as your Guardian
Angel who is assigned to you at birth. All the other Angels and
High Spirit Guides are there when you call upon them for direction. The Universal Realm is ready, willing and able to place you
upon your path of contentment, peace of mind, prosperity and
abundance — yours since birth, by Divine Right.

By not releasing those who attempt to keep you from your
path, brings you "to the hour of your discontent," as Shakespeare
so eloquently wrote. These so called friends, exist in an unhappy
place they are not aware of, but are happy to keep you stuck and
miserable with them. Souls who chose to remain in the dross (a
hypnotized state of not knowing their purpose) and will remain
there until they lift themselves out of the mire of their lives. These
unaware souls are unable to get on with their own lives and have
consciously made the choice not to connect with the powers that
be in the vast recesses of The Universe.

"When you open your heart, you soar like an eagle."

In my practice, I have met people who act like energy vampires. They are the unenlightened souls whom you unintentionally
allow into your life, mostly because you feel sorry for them. Some-

how you delude yourself into thinking you can help them. These dependent souls only know how to take. What they are really doing is draining your life force — a great benefit to them but harmful to you. Energy vampires spend their whole life looking for givers of Love and Light, so they will not have to work to gain their own power, strength and wisdom.

"Friends that are always in need are pests. Let them go!"

I know when someone is acting out in this unenlightened manner within five minutes of being in their space. In the past, it might have taken up to three years of suffering in a relationship before I wised up to what was happening; wondering why I felt so drained after being near them. Now that I am aware of these people I no longer choose to be involved with them.

In the metaphysical realm, there is an ancient society known as the Macro Philosophy Society, consisting of 10 levels of spiritual development. The members of the 10 group are Jesus, Buddha, Krishna and others who have incarnated or work only in the Cosmos as Universal Light Guides and Teachers. The average dedicated teacher of Universal Wisdom is rated six to nine. Then there are the Micros who are at levels one and two — whom I call, 'dim-bulbs.' Dim-bulbs are the unenlightened who are not completely in the dark, but they still have a journey to make in order for them to become fully aware of the wisdom and Light that awaits within.

We are all at the exact level of consciousness *we chose to be*. We do not evolve to the next level unless we make the necessary changes in our thought processes. Prove to yourself that what you feel and believe works when you are tapping into the glorious Universe. When you change, others will notice the change within you; even if you refuse to see it.

"Change is good when it's apparent."

Completely tapping into an all knowing, high system of learning is how I now live my life, and all the stories that you read, reflect that wisdom.

* * * * *

One day in 1989, I was teaching a class on Treasure Mapping. A treasure map is a collection of pictures depicting what we want

manifested for our Highest Good. Just as a road map indicates the
way to a planned destination; treasure maps help us get what we
desire: a healing, a job, possessions, happiness, relationships or any
other wish. Physically, it is piece of paper or board on which we
have placed pictures of what we want along with statements of
faith to remind us that The Universe wants us to have good in our
lives.

With a map comes sureness of possibilities. The making of a
map is an act of belief; a five-step process towards bringing positive
change into your life. According to numerology, the number 5
means change.

The steps are:

1. Intention: Placing what you really want out there.
2. Demonstration: Your willingness to do what is necessary.
3. Realization: Seeing it as it already is, not as you hope it will
   be. Ex.: My book was already a bestseller before it was
   printed.
4. Manifestation: Visualizing and receiving exactly what you
   asked for.
5. Acceptance: Knowing that when your request appears, you
   deserve it and allow it in.

We tend to accept things more readily when we actively do
something towards it. A treasure map keeps all thoughts and pur-
suits moving forward without wasting time, motion, or emotion.

I once created a map on a piece of pasteboard that consisted of
a photo of a grass shack in Hawaii on one side and a picture of a car
on the other. I received both my wishes at the same time, even
though it took a year to manifest. Since than, I have learned how
to sharpen all my senses and now manifest what I want within
seconds of thinking of it.

In 1990, Center Point Project, one of Houston's finest nonprofit teaching facilities, was having a silent auction fund raiser.
There were several items and services donated by practitioners and
members for bidding on. One member had donated a timeshare
trip to Mexico. After reading about the trip, I got an intuitive
message to offer $300. In the past, I would have said that I really
did not want to go there. Now, the new me listens to my inner

voice with its uncanny reasoning. I immediately called and offered $300 for the trip.

There was a get-together a few weeks later, when the auction bidders gathered to hear who had won the donated trips, services and health related items.

I was talking to the lady who had offered the timeshare trip in Mexico, when another woman ran up to me and said, "Tara, you've won the trip to Mexico!"

I looked into the eyes of the woman offering the trip and said, "I really don't want to go to Mexico."

"Where do you want to go?" She asked.

"My dream is to travel to the Hawaiian Islands!" I answered.

"Fine," She said. "I'll call my group and find out if there is a timeshare available."

She called me the next day to tell me there was a condo available on Kauai; one of the smaller Hawaiian islands located next to Oahu where all the other Islanders travel to relax and unwind. *How perfectly, perfect!* Everything turned out, because I 'let go and let God,' guide me to what I wanted most of all!

But the story does not end there!

The Universe has a sense of humor and sometimes it tests our faith. In this case, I was being tested in order to get me to where I really wanted to go, the place of my dreams, the Hawaiian Islands!

The day after I learned I was going to Kauai, I said to myself, "Wouldn't it be great to have a camera to take pictures on my trip?" The next day I received a letter from Mac Haik Chevrolet, a local car dealership. The letter read that they would give me a free 35 mm camera just for test driving their cars. *There was the answer to another request!* I drove to the car lot believing I was going to test drive a car solely with the intent of taking home a camera, but I have since learned there are underlying objectives in the all-knowing realm.

In order for our "requested miracles" to come to pass The Universe must first bring you to those who can guide you (your teachers). Our "request miracles" are so special that The Universe

first has to get us to the location so that what we want comes to pass. This is where the free will stuff comes in — we have a choice, to go or not to go, where we are silently being led.

At the showroom, a swarm of men came towards me. A woman poked her head out from the center of the crowd as she was being pushed from side to side. I thought she would be trampled, but with a strong burst of energy, she pushed her way past the men and walked up to me. I told her that since she showed such persistence, I would like her to help me select the cars to test drive.

We went into her office and she introduced herself as Joan. We talked for a while about the type of car I was looking for. She took me outside and showed me three different cars. The first two I drove did not feel right, but the third, a dark blue Geo-Prism, reminded me of my blessed 1976 dark blue Toyota that had been impounded during a difficult learning experience in Florida. Although I did not come with the intention of purchasing a car; the moment I drove it, I knew I was driving this one home.

Before I left Florida, I had bought a gray 1981 Toyota which I unknowingly released one day while driving the hills of Austin. I did this when I said to myself, "It is time to let you go, Gray, because you no longer have the power needed to climb these small hills." I learned that day to watch what you say or think, as it places the Universal helping wheels in motion, called intention. My Toyota was so reliable that in my heart, I really did not want to release her.

All the events leading up to this moment and coming to the dealership were all a set-up. The Universe knew I needed a new car for future traveling.

Back at the dealership, Joan and I sat down to complete the deal, but just as I was about to sign the contract, I got *new payment jitters* at the thought that since my Toyota was paid for, I would be making payments for another five years. I closed my eyes and asked, "What am I to do now? I am feeling quite overwhelmed with having to start making new car payments all over again." The message I received was, "*Have no fear, the money will always be there.*" Every month, without fail, the monthly car payment came on time, in a variety of unexpected ways!

My old car had sported an "Expect a Miracle" bumper sticker.

I know that you can expect a miracle but you must be willing to recognize it when it happens. I named my new gift from God, "Sapphire Blue Flame of Enlightenment" but I called her "Blue." After I accepted my new car, I made sure this one wore the bumper sticker, "Accept a Miracle," in bold red letters.

Now I had a new car, a camera, and a trip to Kauai. All that was left was to find the $300 to pay for my trip or lose it. On the day my money was due, I found a check in my mailbox for exactly $300!

Before an intervention can take place, the Universe waits until you have finished playing out your trauma dramas. Only after you stop reaching into your fears and limitations can the truth of what is possible, come through.

The last step in this Universal set-up was the manifestation of the plane fare

I located the Capricorn Center, a place of learning on the island, after talking with others who had taught on Kauai. I called and talked with the founder of the center; telling her that I was a teacher and was visiting the island next month. She answered my prayers of how to pay for the trip by saying that she found it divinely interesting that I called just when there was a cancellation exactly the time I was visiting, and would love to have me teach.

Now, I had a condo that was worth $1,500 a week which only cost me $300, the airfare was paid for, and I was ready to embark on a unprecedented learning experience in Kauai. I also gave myself three extra days after Kauai to visit Waikiki, Honolulu on Oahu.

On all my travels, I totally surrender and allow my Guides to show me where they want me to go. By leaving all the details in their capable all knowing Light-hands, I never know what to expect and they know how much I enjoy these miracles. Sometimes I get an even bigger surprise, especially when the trip turns into a "karma-cleanup," such as what happened to me in Kauai.

A sore throat was developing on the way to the airport. It seemed odd since the symptoms had no physical basis that I was aware of. Nonetheless, I arrived in Kauai and was met by Karen, the founder of the Capricorn Center. She was kind enough to meet me at the airport, help me with my rented car and point me in the direction of my condo in the town of Kapaa (pronounced ka-pa-ah). In appreciation for all her kindness, I gave her one of the "harmony balancing necklaces" that I brought to the island to sell to the local shop owners. These are unique necklaces that I am guided to assemble, containing a variety of seven polished stones. After fifteen minutes on the road, I noticed a beautiful mountain and saw what seemed to be a procession of people walking up the mountain. Logically, I knew the image was only in my imagination, but it seemed so real!

I arrived at the condo and not only was my throat getting worse; my nose was also feeling stuffy. I knew from my research that emotional dis-ease when not cleared becomes a disease. My respiratory problems had to do with confusion and stuffing whatever was causing that emotion on a subconscious level. For whatever reason, I was deeply confused and feeling guilty about what I had seen on the mountain.

I was invited to a party later that evening by a neighbor and his wife who were also into the healing arts and knew many of the healers on the island. At the party, I spotted a woman I felt directed to talk with. *"We are always guided to the people we need to meet."* After introducing myself, I shared with her the perplexing scene I had witnessed on the mountain. She told me that mountain was known as *The Mountain of the Dead Kings*, where for centuries, the old and dying kings used to climb, followed by their High Priest and willing subjects, to jump off; as part of a ritualistic way of ending their life cycle, required by tribal laws.

When the lady from the party noticed how all this was affecting me, she told me, to my relief, it was *an honor to die with your king*, thus awakening a past memory. Although it was a tribal law, I felt as their High Priest, I was unwilling to direct my people to, what I believed at that time, was an unnecessary death. I now understood that the band of men that followed me up this mountain, did so for the love of their king and their priest so they would not die alone. This unwillingness to lead people to their death was probably the reason for unresolved guilt and confusion; leading to my symbolic respiratory difficulties from stuffing the emotion.

Once I consciously understood the circumstances behind all she explained, it released a sorrowful energy from my life. I felt better mentally and emotionally, but physically my nose and throat still had not cleared up. I was now losing my voice and there was only a couple of days before my lecture at the Capricorn Center.

Could the fear of standing alone on stage once again be coming back to haunt me?

"We bring into our life that which we fear the most."

While I waited for my class to start, I visited a beautiful Hindu temple on Sunday where I had the pleasure of associating with highly enlightened and loving people. When I saw a half-man half-elephant, marble statue, I asked a monk about it. He said it was a statue of Ganesh, a Hindu prince, who became a symbolic deity when his head was accidentally chopped off by his father, Vishnu, during a hunting trip. (Vishnu is as God-like to India as Zeus is to Greece) When his mother found out, she told Vishnu, *You are a God, bring back my son to me!* Vishnu went back into the woods and took the head of the first animal he spied, which was an elephant. Placing it on his son's body he said that since having the head of an elephant and the body of a man was an obstacle, Vishnu gave Ganesh the power to remove man's obstacles. After hearing this wonderful tale, I sat down to meditate, asking Ganesh to help me remove any obstacles keeping me from my work on the island. Suddenly, I stopped. I felt drawn to look up as an attractive, smiling blond woman walked through the door. I watched as she hugged practically everyone in the temple. I felt I would get to know this enchanting lady soon, but not on this day.

I went back to my meditation, requesting help with an assignment. Before I left for Kauai, I was told to bring six laser crystal healing wands with me and distribute them to certain healing teachers on the island.

These wands appeared to a man I bought my stones and crystals from. He told me that on one of his Quartz Crystal digging expeditions in Hot Springs, Arkansas, he was guided to dig in a out-of-the-way place. There he found 200 crystal wands that he was told were outer-planetary in origin. He told me he was directed to bring them to me and that I would be guided on how, and to whom they would be given to throughout the planet. This mission was easily accomplished with help from the creators of these alien made wands and I am sure, Ganesh in Kauai.

When the Sunday service was over, I left the temple and was led around to the other side where I found a beautiful garden. There I met and talked with an informative man named John. We talked about many other places of interest on the island and he asked if I would like to have lunch with him. I told him I did not date when I travel. The Universe has me on call 24 hours a day and I never know when I am going to be asked to work with someone. He said it did not matter. When I told him that I was teaching on the other side of the island on Wednesday evening, he offered to take me to lunch that day, show me around and drive me to my class, I agreed because I sensed that John would play other parts during my island adventure. Upon finishing our arrangements, I moved on because I felt drawn to talk to a woman who also happened to be a healing teacher. She told me her name was Beth and invited me to her home to continue meditating with a group that met every Sunday after temple. At Beth's place, I took her aside. I felt she would be the one to help me with my mission to distribute the wands, since she knew so many people. She looked at all six, picking one out. After holding it for a minute, she knew that one was hers. She said that she had seen a wand like this in a dream a few days before and she would be made a gift of it. I told her it would be hers if she helped me find the owners of the other four. (I only gave her four because I was told I would meet the owner of the last one later on in the week.) She happily agreed, allowing me more time to meet others on my synchronistic path.

When the day came for me to speak at the Capricorn Center, I barely had a voice left. I closed my eyes and asked, "When I speak, may they hear 'Your' words with an open heart and mind." This is known in some circles as channeling. Channeling is when the words come from your Higher Self or in another voice from your Guides. (I read in the book *Women of the Bible Speak to Women of Today* by Dorothy Elder, that when Moses channeled God's Ten Commandments on Mt. Sinai, it was called, 'speaking voices.') I also knew Ganesh would be helping remove any obstacles. I began to speak but it was not my voice. Some in the class told me that my voice (or that of my Guide) sounded like it had a Minnesota Dutch accent with its distinct O's. This was my first experience in voice channeling. Time passed quickly and we were all surprised when we were out of time.

After class, I asked my Guides where I should go to eat. The message I got was to go to the fast food restaurant located directly across from my condo. Well, I am not impressed with fast food, but I followed their lead and went. I ordered a bowl of soup and walked to the back room where I noticed two women sitting at a table engaged in deep conversation. Before I left on my trip I was told, "Those with crystals will be your guide." Much to my amazement one of the women was wearing a crystal! I introduced myself and told them why I was on the island. The woman wearing the crystal said that I had arrived at a perfect time, because one of the island's Aunties (Auntie is a common name given to respected teachers on the islands) was giving a demonstration the following evening, on a hands on healing technique called, "Lomi Lomi," which translates to 'loving the body.' She said if I would like to attend, she would be happy to give me a ride. This sounded great. My body was in need of a special healing to love it into feeling better.

"A massage is a message of love to the body."

When we arrived, I recognized the blonde lady from the temple sitting in the audience. During the class, Auntie Grace asked for a volunteer and the blonde lady's hand shot up. Auntie looked directly at her and said, "You are the one I choose." At the end of the demonstration, the blonde came over to our group and asked the woman who had brought me if she would take her home. In the car, she told me that she intuitively knew Auntie would choose her to participate, even before she arrived. She told me her spiritual name was Aguilla and she was a massage therapist from Germany. When she first came to the islands, she lived in Maui for five years but was drawn to the tranquillity and spirituality of Kauai. She said that she lives in a tent on a beach known as 'Hidden Beach.' I felt an instant friendship with this free spirited woman. She asked if I would like to go sightseeing with her and a friend the next day and I happily agreed. When Aguilla called for me at my condo, I was surprised to see her with John, the man I met at the temple. According to her, they dated off and on. We drove to her home on Hidden Beach, a secret strip of beach not open to the public and not easily found unless you are shown the only en trance. Near the entrance to the beach, we met another friend of Aguilla standing next to his truck loaded with coconuts. She told me he was the resident authority on the gestation process of coco-nuts. I looked at her as if to say, "Is this for real?" I asked him what the big deal was, about the aging process of coconuts. Seriously, he told me that there was more to coconuts than just cutting one open and eating it. Coconuts are like fine wine, he said. You have to understand the ripening stages to know when to eat them for their variety of tastes. I listened as her friend happily went on and on, explaining that the longer a coconut ripens, the more fermented it becomes. I felt like I was at a wine tasting session for coconuts! The first few tasted bland, but they got progressively sweeter and potent. By the time we got to the last one, it was like drinking pure alcohol! When we finally got to the entrance, the 'mega-proof' coconut definitely helped me relax as we started our climb down a small mountainside leading to the beach. Holding on to tree branches for balance was the only thing that kept me from slipping on all the slimy crushed kumquats that lined the steep path. When we finally reached the bottom, much to my surprise, the beach was inhabited by free-spirited nudists. The residents camped out in tents and showered in only cold water that flowed nonstop from a thin metal pipe jutting out from the side of the mountain. This section of the island, with a lighthouse overlooking the horizon, was pristine and unspoiled, even with the size of the population and the number of tents laid out in the sand. I felt completely at ease as I walked nude alongside my new friends and the other unencumbered tent dwellers.

Aguilla wrote me months later telling me how disappointed she was that she had to leave her tent home because the beach was no longer a "hidden" secret, catering to the nude and famous.

Shakti Gawain, whose house overlooks Hidden Beach, told me years later at a conference, steps had been constructed leading safely down the mountain.

While on the island, I visited many stores, talking with shop owners who were interested in buying my "harmony-balancing necklaces." Since I brought only a few necklaces, I sold them directly to the owners. My reason being, if a store owner saw how great they looked and felt, they would order them. One owner who had purchased a necklace, called me the following day and told me that the owner of a health food store had seen her wearing it, loved the unusual design and wanted to buy one as a birthday gift for his wife. I returned to the woman's shop and met with the health food store owner. I showed him my last necklace and asked him if he would be interested in it for his wife. "No," He said. "I want the one around your neck!" I told him that particular necklace was from my personal collection and not for sale. He insisted that he had to have that specific necklace for his wife. I intuitively asked him where his wife was from and he replied, "Texas!" Now, I ask you, how could I possibly say no to a man whose wife was from my home state of Texas? I knew that she was meant to wear the necklace that I had enjoyed for more than five years.

A few hours before I left for Honolulu, I had the opportunity to visit with Auntie Grace at her beautiful retreat where she practiced and taught Lomi Lomi, as she had demonstrated days before.

Lomi Lomi massage therapy consists of dipping your body into an ice-cold swimming pool followed by meditation and massage. (Cold water represents death of the old ways or feelings.) After the dip you walk to another area to sit facing a sacred mountain on the horizon, where during meditation, you send all your stored anger and emotions for a wonderful release. Next, you lie on a massage table in a small cabin which contains a rock chamber that sends wafts of aromatic steam through the room, as you are lovingly massaged by Auntie and two highly intuitive practitioners. All three steps are repeated every thirty minutes or until your emotional body has released whatever it needs for your Highest Good at that time. The whole procedure takes a minimum of two hours, but time only permitted me one. I traded her the last laser healing wand for this session. She told me that she knew, at first glance, this wand was meant for her to use on her clients in conjunction with Lomi Lomi.

We have many layers of negative energy stuck within the body since childhood. When you release this energy too quickly your mind and body is unable to cope with this insult. Loving techniques such as Lomi Lomi and Reiki allow the body to release these layers from the past or present, in a more loving and harmonious way.

At the airport, I thanked all my Guides for helping to make all these super connections. I boarded the plane and left behind, only for now, the lush play land island of Kauai and anticipating the next wondrous insights waiting to be revealed to me in Honolulu, only 45 minutes away as the eagle flies. While on board, I said to my Guides, "I'm physically feeling much better now since most of the great healers of the island have spiritually loved my body, so to speak, so how about more fun and less work?" The answer was, "How about some fun with a modicum of work?"

The first day on Waikiki was mine to enjoy. I chose to lounge on the beach admiring the sights of a place I envisioned as "God's Earthly Heaven." When I returned to my room, I heard a message in my mind that said, "Go to the library." I asked myself why would I want to go to *a library?* I remembered that not everything from our Guides is meant to be taken literally. I was guided to the hotel across the street from mine and on one of the lobby billboards it read, "The Library." It turns out this message was referring to a small nightclub inside the hotel. I surmised that I was being guided to someone who was in need of help, and who in turn, would help me with the 'having some fun part' as my Guides had mentioned.

I took the elevator to the 4th floor where the bar was located. Standing in front of the club, I noticed an easel which held a framed picture of the entertainers; a man playing the piano and a woman singing. I felt it was the woman I was to meet. Since the bar would not be open for another hour, I decided to treat myself to a healing session with a Shiatsu practitioner on the same floor. Shiatsu is a Japanese form of deep finger pressure on the meridians pathways of the body. After my treatment, I went back to the club, walked up to the bar, and sat down. On the next stool sat a woman with her back to me, listening to the piano player. I tapped her on the shoulder, and she turned around. I recognized her as the woman singer I had seen in the ad. It was no surprise when I saw that she was wearing a crystal! (Remember the phrase "Those with crystals will be your guide?") I introduced myself and explained that I was a spiritual intuitive advisor that had been brought to this bar to meet and help her sort out some type of problem. She said her name was Carole and it was fate that I appeared because she and her husband were not getting along and hardly talking. I listened, as she told me of the problems they were having. She said that they had an album to cut so she certainly could use my help. I explained to her that I would be willing to show her how to improve their relationship in exchange for her guiding me through the sights of Honolulu. That night, she informed her husband that she needed three days off in order to work with me. He was not at all pleased with her request and reminded her that they still needed to re-hearse for the album. She told him she needed my help in dealing with their problems and rehearsals would have to wait or there would be no album. We talked further about how I could be of assistance to her and she made an appointment to come to my hotel room the following morning.

I worked with her in the hotel for the three days I stayed in Waikiki. One of the problems I helped Carole understand was why her husband was acting unusually grouchy and bossy during their rehearsals. The information I received was "To him, time is money and being the perfectionist that he is, he wants everything to go right. Since rehearsals have not gone to his liking, he needs to lash out at someone. As uncomfortable as it seems right now, you're it." When the message was completed, I explained to her about the Touching the Lion on the Nose meditation and she gladly let me guide her through it.

In the mornings we completed a session, and in the afternoons we went sightseeing. One place she took me to was a dormant volcano filled with ocean water. Carole brought her snorkeling gear and I had my first snorkeling experience. You could not walk into the water because of the sharp rocks, so you had to belly flop in. Brightly colored fish swam up and allowed me to touch them. I suggested to Carole that we discharge a 'Primal Scream,' a cleans-ing ritual created by Arthur Janov, Ph.D., to help release any pent-up emotions coming from the depth of our soul. I thought the releasing aspect would work even better in water since water in itself is cleansing. After screaming under water, we opened our eyes and watched as we were surrounded by a large cascade of bubbles. We felt great but noticed that we scared off the fish. I telepathically sent out an apology to our fish friends and they quickly swam back for more attention.

In the evenings we ate dinner laughing like two old friends, and then onto the bar where I sang along with Carole and her husband until closing.

One evening while in the bar, the manager of one of the other restaurants in the hotel, came in and told me Carole said that I did hands on healing. When I told him that was correct he wanted to know if I would help his best waiter who was in pain and could hardly walk. I asked him what the problem was. He said that the waiter told him that one day, for no reason, his knee started hurting. The pain had become much worse and was now affecting his work. I went to the restaurant, and he brought me to the waiter, who was sitting in a chair almost in tears from the pain. I placed my hands on his knee and I received a message to ask the waiter about his dog. He said that his dog had died the week before. I asked him when the pain started. He looked at me as if a light had just gone off and he said that the pain had started the day after his dog died. I asked him to describe the relationship he had with his dog. He said that his dog was his best friend, because he was always there for him and the best company.

Domesticated animals sense the needs of their owners and their purpose in life is to make their human companions happy. The waiter told me that in his human relationships, everybody left him. When his dog left, it was too much for him to take and the loss created an emotional void in his heart and a deep depression that translated into the dis-ease within his knee.

The knees are the area of the body relating to not moving forward with ease. When he told me he understood how his emotional feelings manifested the pain, I told him to get up and walk. He stood up and moved around without any pain.

> *"When an owner uses an animal's love in place of a*
> *humans, a deep feeling of loss and emotional*
> *devastation can ensue after the animal dies."*

When I returned home, Carole wrote that she was amazed that after each of our sessions, her attitude changed towards her husband and he also changed, becoming less and less uptight about the upcoming album. They had worked out all their disagreements, finished their album and were once again singing lovebirds. Carole and her husband found out the answers to all their questions because they were ready and open to recognize — there was a problem.

> *"Knowing why you are doing what you do, leads you*
> *to finding your answers."*

As you read the stories throughout this book, you can see how I have allowed an invisible Universal Guidance System to lead me to the places I need to be, easily and effortlessly. Know that we can all use this invaluable system, whether it comes from our Higher Self, the Angelic Realm or from our Personal Guides. The Universal Realm is invaluable when you permit it to help you everyday and in every way, as I do. In return, they will gladly show you how to get the most out of life on planet Earth.

A point of intervention information. The camera that got me to the car dealer never really worked. Or did it?

Chapter 4

Listen To Your Body, Mind, Spirit and Language

When you listen to your *whole being*, you will know exactly what it needs and wants

One day I had a strong craving for root beer; a strange thing for me. I do not remember the last time I drank root beer or anything carbonated, since I heard that carbonated bubbles can remain trapped in your intestines. So, I went to the health store and was drawn to the sassafras and sarsaparilla herbs in the bulk section. Their combined smells seemed familiar but I could not place it. I asked a sales lady what she thought and she said they both smelled strangely like *root beer!* Curious, I looked up their medicinal properties in an herb book. It said they were blood purifiers and cleansers for the skin. Detoxifying was exactly what I needed at the time, since red bumps had erupted on my face while on one of my trips. The solution to my problem came to me because of my strong desire to heal, thus guiding me in the exact direction for the cure.

Before retiring one night, I had a craving for red meat, which is unusual because I do not enjoy eating it. That night in a dream, I was served a plate of beef stew. I told the server that I wanted chicken instead. The next evening a friend took me to a cafeteria for dinner; among the choices I noticed one small bowl of beef stew. I thought about the dream and seeing this bowl of stew was too much of a coincidence for me to ignore it. As I ate the badly prepared chunks of meat that tasted like it had been sitting there all day, I knew I really did not want it. A part of me still refused to eat meat. The dream was telling me I needed protein even though I had been eating proteins in other forms, such as soy and algae.

When you have a craving for something that you normally do not eat, surrender to it; for whatever reason your body wants it. If it disturbs you to eat it, not to worry, all can be released from the body by using fiber cleansers: Cascara Sagrada, Plantago Psyllium seed (blonde), Black Walnut bark (kills parasites from the meat) and Senna Pod. For a liver cleanse, see Appendix V.

The body will tell you what it needs, unless of course it is a sugar carbohydrate addiction attack and you eat a whole box of chocolates. When you desire sweets, and you find yourself *eating the whole thing*, ask yourself what emotions are you *stuffing* and *what is not sweet in my life?* Search for any emotional stresses that occurred in the last 48 hours. Love yourself enough to get answers before your body suffers from excessive use of sweets.

"Change toxic eating behaviors before they are catapulted from your 'open mouth insert food receptacle,' creating an eating disorder."

Understanding Your Emotional Bodies
Our emotional states of anger, hate, sadness and disappointment, play a big role in creating physical ailments.

Since everything contains energy, there is a correlation between your material possessions and your emotional bodies or your five subtle bodies.
1. Physical = Your home
2. Mental = Your home
3. Emotional = Your car
4. Spiritual = Your garden
5. Etheric = Your Universal intuition

Home = physical and mind
A client shared an incident when both her washing machine and air conditioner broke down within the same day. I explained the correlation between her washing machine and her life. Since the main function of her washing machine was to clean out the dirt, I asked her what was not running properly in her life so she could "clean up her act." It turned out it was her life that was not working. She kept bringing men into her life who were 'taking her to the cleaners' with the results that she was "broke" all the time!

Regarding her air conditioner, I asked her what was not "cool" in her life; was she "hot under the collar," possibly over an angry situation that remained unresolved? She told me that was exactly the way her life had been and she appeared astounded that it took the breaking down of her appliances to shake her up to the fact that her life was in shambles and it had to change!

Car = emotional

My father bought me a 1964 burgundy Chevy Impala for my high school graduation gift. The first weekend I drove the car, I was hit in the driver's side door by a woman who ran a stop sign. That was just the beginning of an unforgettable day. On the way to find out how much the accident cost, I was in another one!

It was not until years later, during a meditation session, did I understand how and why this unconscious energy was played out.

Due to unresolved issues of feeling unloved by my father, I took my anger out on my car — my emotional body. As I attempted to destroy what felt uncomfortable, receiving a car in lieu of love from my father, this time, I was *jolted into a conscious awareness and slammed into reality*, concerning my true feelings. I was outwardly demonstrating, "If I can't have your love, Dad, I don't want this car, a poor substitute."

"We are all co-conspirators in life's emotional plays."

Instead of resolving the issues and facing my father about how I felt, I continued to take my anger out on the car and had three more accidents, all within a year. Two mishaps in the rear, (I guess I needed a good swift bump in the rear to get my attention) and one by another woman running a stop sign. Yes, the operative word was STOP! After the last accident, my father decided that the car was no longer safe for me to drive, so, he sold it to a friend who drove it for over 12 years. *Since he had no emotional issues with the car, he had no accidents or problems whatsoever!*

Another way Dad's gift pulled on my emotional strings was, if I did not come home when my mother wanted me to, she threatened to have my father take away the car. One day, I had enough of her telling me what time she wanted me home so I gave her the keys and left home at 17. I chose to run away instead of facing my unhappy situation; though having since learned to face my lions. I left home because I wanted to make the point that,

"A gift is not a gift when there are strings."

Also I did not want their car, as much as I wanted to *feel* their love. Sometimes, I still want to run away when faced with bossy, controlling people, but I know now that,

"Running away does not get you anywhere;
facing your obstacles will."

When I look back, I understand what was really going on in the scheme of things. My father was showing me his love in his normal materialistic way. My mother wanted to keep me safe with her own form of discipline. All I know is that I *would have traded that beautiful new car for a hug or simply an "I love you."*

Plants/garden = spiritual body

During a recent flight to Vancouver, B.C., Canada, a woman happened to mention to me during casual conversation, that her once beautiful garden was dying. I felt there was more to this story. (I love the investigative part of my work!) I asked her to tell me what had been going on in her life before her plants started to wilt. It seems her husband had recently died and she wanted to die too.

Because of depression and lack of energy, she no longer wanted to take care of a garden that had once brought her so much comfort and pleasure. Now it was *withering*. I told her that as soon as she returned home, go straight to her garden and talk with the protectors of Mother Nature's Realm; the Devas and Fairies that watch over it. Ask them how she could make her plants healthy again, look to The Universe and ask for peace in getting past this unhappy time in her life.

After I returned home, she called and told me that both the garden (the spiritual body) and her peace of mind (home life) had miraculously revived and she felt more like living.

When she made the decision to follow a stranger's suggestion, she allowed herself to connect with the message I brought her, possibly from her husband, that helped set her free from her feelings of loss. If she had not been open to the message, she might have chosen to end her life and once again be with her beloved partner.

* * * * *

In February of 1998, during my first pre-publishing party that the *Indigo Sun* magazine sponsored, Allan Perkins, a writer and friend, walked into the party holding a plant and said, "May this plant grow as your book grows." I took the plant home and a week later a beautiful pink flower bloomed. (Pink is the color of unconditional love.) The flower went through its life cycle and the three tall green leaves surrounding the flower remained and continued to grow. Before leaving on a three week tour of the West Coast, I asked a client to water my plants and she promised she would. When I returned, all my leafy plants were dead. My aloe vera plants were the sole survivors. I threw all the dead ones away except for the book plant because I could not part with it. It appeared dead, but to me, it represented the continuation of my book; if the plant was gone, bad luck could follow. Nine months later at the beginning of winter and after locating the perfect team for the completion of this book, the plant miraculously started growing again, normally an amaryllis' dormant stage. It was as though the plant had a rebirth of sorts, and came back as soon as my book was back on track. I am so glad that I listened to whomever kept me from throwing away a plant that on the surface appeared to be a lost cause. This was how I was feeling about my book at the time; especially after I found out how much it would cost to self-publish, until I got the message to have pre-publishing parties and pre-sell them. Pre-selling afforded me the income to continue. Thanks to lots of help from 'the kindness of strangers,' my book was not just a dream or a desire any longer. Everything worked out in Divine Order, because before *Universe On The Move* went to press, I pre-sold almost 200 books throughout the United States and Canada.

These stories help to explain a profound connection between our subtle bodies and that miracles will always be a part of our life when we are open and receptive to The Universe's help. Being fully open will help you to understand that what you believe with your mind and not your Higher Self, is not always the way towards finding your answers. By using your "Higher Love Heart" and The Universal Guides who are the true experts of God's Realm, you will be led to all you need to know.

"Nothing is as it seems in the all knowing Universal Realm."

As the answers to underlying causes concerning any and all of your so called dilemmas unfold for your understanding, you will once again re-connect with the Holy Spirit. When you choose not to use this method, you are tantamount to being disconnected from God and all the Glory that is yours by Divine Right. *Your choices are connected or disconnected — the decision is yours.*

When you fully understand the connection of your subtle bodies to the happenings in your life, you will experience what is really going on in the Grand Universal Plan and the nature of things to come. This also involves the mechanics of Universal Cause and Effect, also described as, "Reap what you sow," or, " What you put out into the Cosmos will come back to you tenfold."

"It does not take long for the give and take of karmic action to occur when you are willing to open to this Cosmic way of life."

A positive example of karma in action/reaction mode

When I was teaching at Center Point, a woman bought one of my prosperity bags containing eight gemstones, an animal fetish and three affirmations, created through guidance, to teach prosperity consciousness. All millionaires have this consciousness and without it you will not prosper. When the customer paid me the ten dollars for the bag, I asked her "Are you willing for the money you gave me to come back to you ten fold?" When she said yes, I continued with, "Are you now ready and willing to accept and receive all the bounty The Universe wants to give you, with no exceptions?" Again she said yes. I ended with, "So be it. Praise God." She left and I went back to work. Two hours later I received a phone call from the customer who had purchased the prosperity bag earlier in the day. She was crying. Between sobs, she said, that she played a scratch off game and won $1,000!

The ever powerful Ego

Remember, your body-mind is always listening to what you say, but your Ego needs you to be happy. The Ego has to prove that what you say is right, and does this by using your every word, phrase, or action, *when you give the Ego permission to have the last word.* Our Ego was originally meant for our protection in a logical way; to stop us when we were in trouble or on the path of destruction. When we chose not to take responsibility for running our own lives, we gave our power over to the Ego. For example, if you were to step out in front of a moving truck, our original Ego might say, "Danger, watch out for that truck." Now that we have given it so much power, when you walk into danger you may hear the Ego yell, "What are you blind?! Didn't you see the truck?! Why don't you watch where you're going?!" Your Ego sounds more judgmental than helpful. I once heard Reverend Howard Caesar of The Unity Church in Houston mention during a lesson, that Ego is an acronym for *"Edging God Out."*

Changing Your Toxic Vocabulary

I strongly understand, "we are what we say, think, feel, believe and eat." It stands to reason that it is important to watch the words and phrases we use. We continually speak negatively, having unwittingly copied our parents, teachers, and the friends we associate with. Whether we know it or not, we continually say things that we are not consciously aware of. Mostly we say things as a defensive mechanism from times not yet healed. For example, we want to tell someone what we really feel, but instead of staying in our power, we change it to, *Oh, I was only kidding,* so not to hurt their feelings. That person will never know what we really wanted to convey was important to us. By acting this way, we hide our true feelings and remain in our emotional pain. As far as dealing with anger, we uncontrollably lash out after we have been hurt, whether verbally cutting down another or through physical abuse. Most of the time we are not even aware why we reacted in the first place, but your inner child certainly knows!

"A situation, problem, pain, or emotional upset appears to help us look at and understand what is really going on in our lives."

I have compiled a list of negative and positive statements which we all have used at one time or another, during our toxic vocabulary era. Using a negative combination of words is known as an oxymoron. Speaking in oxymorons seems moronic to me. Also nonproductive, if you want to stay in your power. Statements like, *awfully good* or *terribly happy.* Well, is it awful or is it good? How can it be both? Decide which way suits you — good and happy definitely get my vote.

These are phrases I wholeheartedly recommend releasing; they are not empowering:

I would really die for a piece of cake! Come on, would you really die for anything so trivial? It is possible that you might have problems from eating too many sweets.

I don't have the time. You certainly find the time when you are doing what you enjoy the most or when helping others. Repeat three times: *I am the Master of time, time is not my Master!*

It's incredible. Such as 'It's incredible I won a trip to Kauai.' What you are really saying is, *it's not credible,* I never win anything!

I really lucked out. I feel that phrase definitely needs to be switched to I really *lucked in.* When something great happens it means you are *in luck,* not, *out of luck.*

She can't come to the phone because she's tied up. What a unpleasant picture that brings to mind. A body bound by obstacles without the freedom to do what it wants. By using this phrase, you are verbally not permitting yourself to move forward or have the life you really want.

Using the word *just,* as in, *I'm just a housewife.* You are not *just* anything. You are all that there is or will be. Placing 'just' in front of who you are, tends to diminish, all you can be.

Constantly saying *I'm sorry.* Stop being and feeling sorry for yourself and the world's problems! By using *I'm sorry* often, denotes a time when you wept those soulful words as a child. Every time you use these words, it brings back the same feelings of, what, "I'm sorry" may have stood for while growing up, like, *I didn't mean it!* or *It's all my fault!* An empowering way to use 'I'm sorry' that keeps you out of your 'poor me state' is *'I'm sorry' that happened to you* or

I'm sorry that you feel that way. If you use "I'm sorry" to be polite, say "excuse me" instead. This way you own "I'm sorry" and it does not own you.

I'm going crazy or *You're driving me crazy.* Let that road be the one less traveled.

You're giving me a headache. I have had clients tell me if they just got rid of their spouses, children or the job they hate, their headaches would go away. *It is time to start taking responsibility for your own stuff and stop blaming others!*

I don't want to hear it, a commonly used phrase. A client once told me she used that phrase whenever her children were complaining about a sibling, and she was losing her hearing. She went to medical doctors seeking answers but they could not explain the loss of her hearing until she understood, *we really are what we say!*

Leave me alone. When using this phrase, those in your life may help with what you ask for, which is to **leave you**.

One day I was working with a client and throughout the whole conversation of her berating her parents, she repeated "I was so stupid. Why was I so stupid? I can't believe how stupid I was." When she finished with this 'stupid monologue' I said, "Do you realize that you have repeated how stupid you were at least five times, within a five minute story about your family?" She answered, "I did?" On a conscious level, my client never *heard* herself saying the word. I find that most people do not really listen to what they say. I discovered that the reason she constantly called herself stupid was, as a child, her parents, teachers and friends called her that. This reinforces the feelings it represented that she held deep within her subconscious which she unknowingly claimed as her truth. Even though she earned a Ph.D., all she ever *felt* was stupid.

When you have made the decision to go outside the Universal Realm for help with an emotional problem, you are ready to let go; seek out a counselor who can intuitively help you. Someone who will listen for your negative phrases and actions, in order to quickly help you move past them.

"Releasing all negativity is the pathway to freedom."

In my practice, I find the quickest way to help someone is to bring their negative vocabulary and the emotional attachment that it stimulates immediately to their attention. When they are feeling the emotion, I ask them to go back to a person or time when this feeling first came into their life. Through meditative exercises, they can get in touch with whomever or whatever and face it. This method has helped clients move through their baggage and imprints in a most expedient way.

"Replace unwanted messages with positive ones."

The use of emotionally charged words take their toll on you and those around you. It is important to hear what you say to others. Your voice is a vibrational weapon and if that vibration comes out in a volatile manner, it will have harmful repercussions on the sender as well as the receiver. By using this exercise, you will learn how to get in touch with the negative side of your inner turmoil to let it go.

"You are what you say, think, feel, believe and eat!"

To help my clients become more aware of what verbally or mentally must be changed in order for them to move on to a better life, I ask them to say, "I now give myself permission to hear and change the toxic negative words, phrases, and sentences I say to myself, and others, that are not for my Highest Good, or theirs. So be it. Praise God." I tell them once they have given themselves permission, they will hear the words needed to be changed in their mind before they utter them. If you occasionally find yourself still spouting verbal negativities, say, "cancel cancel" and rephrase it into something positive. This technique is also known as reprogramming; a method I learned during a Silva Mind Method class taught by Wanda Morris.

A much quicker way to learn what your negative words are would be to ask your friends or co-workers to help. I am sure they would be ecstatic assisting you with this worthy goal. They probably know these phrases better than you, since they *have listened* to you repeat them often enough.

Would you rather be happy or would you rather be right?

When I ask this during a class or session, there are always a few in the group who say they want to be *both*, they need to be right about being right! Instead of negotiating peace, people have fought wars and died to be right. I know that I want to be happy, but I get paid to be correct.

"Allowing yourself to be happy is better than having to be right."

How Our Language Controls Us

I have often asked people what they are doing to make their life better. One answer I often hear is, "I'm waiting until I win the lottery then everything will be perfect." My response is, "What other excuse did you use before the lottery, that kept you from moving on with your life?" Instead of hoping to win the lottery, use your "God Given Wisdom," and tune into creating a better way of life. I have met many millionaires who know that money alone does not bring happiness. Instead of believing everything will be great, only after you have enough money, time or find the right partner; believe instead that when you are happy you will bring in all you want and more. Learn the causes of your problems instead of going through your life wondering. Wondering only touches the surface of why bad things happen to good people. An insightful way to ask your questions of the Universe would be: *What's going on? What does this mean? How did that happen?* and *I am ready for my answers now!*

Our thinking and language affect us, negatively, when we are unaware of the ramifications of misusing certain words and phrases. **First** are the *Ifs*. This small two-letter word can keep you from your power of thought and lead to procrastination. I wish I had a nickel for every time I used that small rascal of a word in a sentence. I used to say to myself, "If only I had professed my love to John when I was 16, I would not, continue, to beat myself up about what might have been!"

While visiting with Maria Papapetros a psychic consultant, she looked me straight in the eyes and said, "Who is John?" I told her he was the first and only love of my life. She replied most emphatically, "Let him go!" She was the first person who helped me see what I knew in my heart but refused to listen to. I finally got the message and recognized that everything happens for a reason.

Giving pertinent information like Maria gave me about John, is an excellent sign of a true psychic messenger, unlike those who tell you that you are cursed and it will take thousands of dollars to have it removed. A legitimate intuitive, working within the 'Celestial White Light Realm,' would never act in this manner. These are the *charlatans and thieves* that have caused those needing the guidance of teachers and healers of God's True Light to be afraid to seek us out. I have had many a frightened person come to me for help because they were more afraid of the curse than the original problem that caused them to seek help in the first place.

After these so called psychics had been documented duping the public by the news media, they still claimed, right in front of the camera, that they help people. They believe their own lies; that they are really relieving people of their emotional pain. I have been told by those they had duped that the only thing they relieved them of was their money! This is a good example of why it is more efficient and practical to seek help from the all knowing Light Realm, than to ask those that may be *more in the dark* about your problem.

> *"Not all that is seen by the naked eye is gospel*
> *in the all knowing realm"*

Second of the commonly used negative words are the *buts;* the true reason for procrastination. *I'm going to, but ... I should, but... I want to, but...I was thinking about doing it, but ...* (my favorite) and the most used, *I'm trying to, but ...* What you need to do is, *get off* using but, and you will get off *your butt.*

Do whatever it is you believe you can not do, in spite of the reasons you chose to believe why you could not do it. *Just do it anyway.* If you understand this in any way, shape or form, you got it 'made in the shade.'

Third, *can't* means *won't* and if you *won't,* why *can't* you? There is an expression that states "stop second-guessing yourself." Instead of asking others *why did this have to happen to me,* placing you once again in your poor-me state, ask the empowering questions, *What does this mean? What are these circumstance bringing to my attention? Help me to better understand what is really going on?* And finally, *I am now ready to know the true meaning of my actions, I want my answers now!*

Find the underlying causes of all your misconscrewtions (a made-up word) which means 'one who has a screwed-up form of communication.'

The perfect time to state any of the above inquiries to your Guides is before going to sleep. Also ask that you will remember your dreams upon waking. When you wake-up, you only have about 30 seconds left in the Alpha state, the meditative place just before sleep, for acute memory recall. Ask yourself quickly upon arising, what was this dream telling me? Be specific when asking questions or you may not get the precise answers. Question everything and know these lessons will help you learn from the mistakes that exist in a life that you were brought here to complete — always in an easy and effortlessly manner.

"There is always a lesson within the lessons."

When I work with a client who chooses to repeat the words *I know* after practically every one of my suggestions, I usually tell them if they know everything I am suggesting, explaining or advising, they do not need me or anyone else to reinforce what they claim they already know. Instead, say you do not know, show me the way and the answers will always come. When I used to say "I know," but did not have a clue, there was no reason for The Universe to answer me since I was not asking a question or for their help. Now when I want to know, I look up into the heavens and say, *"I don't know what to do with this problem, I am stuck so I give it up to you. Please guide me to the answers that are for my Highest Good and soul growth."* By surrendering my problems and giving all up to Sweet Spirit, something better will manifest itself.

"When in doubt surrender; give it up and let it go."

CHAPTER 5

Past Life Connections

We are part of a group consciousness; connected telepathically with those from our past. Therefore, when you receive an inner feeling or message, *"Your first thought is the true connection to your Higher Self or the Astral Plane."*

We often ignore our first intuitive feelings. These thoughts or feelings are based on our Higher Intuitive Self and are the ones to act upon. Everything that follows is your left brain or analytical side, telling you that message could not possibly be correct because the answer came too easily.

"We are not smart enough to make up feelings and messages from Universal Spirit Guides; trust those first Cosmic answers."

When there are problems in this life, and events we really do not understand, enjoy, or feel good about, there is usually an underlying cause. A pesky negative energy force from a past life existence needing to be released or a malevolent energy force that has no idea it is no longer wanted or needed as a part of this incarnation. If you do not believe in reincarnation, Einstein proved that energy does not die, it just changes and the energy from our ancestors are part of our cellular make-up, containing a history of past energy activity. We may have the same feelings and thoughts as some of our ancestors; even being drawn to certain occupations or people, whether negatively or positively. Mozart is a good example, playing piano at three and composing at five. However, we may be completely unaware that this energy exists, and could be the reason for any strange or unanswerable actions on our part. They also trigger patterns and addictions, keeping us from being who we were meant to be or want to be; the perfect relationship, job or just getting on with our life.

I learned about two interesting past incidents with the help of a traveling metaphysical teacher named Beatrice.

I never really understood why the physical act of sex was always painful to me. During a past life regression, I tuned into a life where I had been kidnapped and repeatedly raped by marauders during a 17th century war. Throughout the long days and longer nights, I prayed to be released from my unbearable pain. This horror and humiliation lasted about a month before my pleadings for death were finally answered.

Understanding this long forgotten past life memory helped me to understand and release the cause of why I did not enjoy sex.

After helping me remember this past life, Beatrice suggested that I begin working with the Diva Realm. (Personal, friendly spirits who help when asked.) She told me whenever she finished a session, she would call upon her Diva to tell her how much to charge, especially if she went over the allotted time. She informed me that I had a Diva named Greta who wanted to help me in the same way. After hearing the name Greta, a peculiar sensation came over me. I remembered feeling the same way when I had heard that Greta Garbo had died. Beatrice noticed me shivering and asked me, "What are you seeing and feeling right now?" I said, "I see many scarves waving in the air." She told me that I had lived in the time of John the Baptist.

"I am receiving the name, "Salome." I said. (A good teacher does not tell you everything, but allows you to form your own conclusions, and helps only if you get stuck.)

"You were the mother of Salome, and Greta Garbo was Salome." She told me.

"That would make me the wife of King Herod!" I said. *"YUK!"*

Salome (Greta) and I, as her mother Herodias, (marrying the masculine name to yours; a coincidence?) were all part of a Divine plan involving Jesus and his mission on Earth during the 'times that try men's souls.' I was informed by Beatrice that the reason all this information was resurfacing now was, because Greta Garbo had not yet ascended into God's Light. Her essence was in limbo, unaware that it was time to go to the Light! I was told, by my Guides, to tune into her soul and share these words with her, *"Greta, you were to John, as Judas was to Jesus!"* The moment she received this ethereal message into her soul process, there came a healing and a great release for both of us. I knew on some level, that I was connected to Jesus' death on some level. I did not know until that day that my part had to do with John, Salome and Herod and that is why Greta's release was also a release to me!

Like Salome, Greta was also a performer. In this life, due to the tremendous guilt from her participation in the beheading of John, she most likely could not tolerate being in large groups; hence her isolation from life. It is a miracle that, with all her karmic pain, she did not commit suicide but instead opted to drop out of the limelight

I was happy I could help Greta during her final journey home.

* * * * *

As a result of unresolved negative energy from the past, I have had clients tell me they feel uncomfortable wearing anything that touched their neck. I asked guidance what could be causing this problem and I received, "Those are the ones who have been harmed around the head area, brought about by past indiscretions causing them to be hung, strangled or decapitated."

To help them, I have been guided to place both my hands around their neck and say, "I reconnect with the past life that is causing your distress. It doesn't matter what the cause of the problem, are you now willing to let go of this unwanted energy?" When they answer "Yes," they are then free from the incarnation causing their discomfort.

"It doesn't matter if you do not understand the cause of your distress, just be willing to let it go."

I have also had clients come to me with a fear of water, heights or confined places. I tell them the problem could be caused by a bit of left over energy residue not yet released from childhood or stuck within the body, on a cellular level, from a particular incarnation.

When there are problems or events in our life we really do not understand, enjoy or feel good about, there is always an underlying cause. If negative energy has not been released *before incarnation,* it may be because it still has issues remaining to resolve from the last poor-me syndrome addiction, with its soul remembered benefits or payoffs. When we are unhappy, we have a tendency not to do anything, keeping us depressed and stuck. This gives us a good excuse not to do something, instead of finding out what the original problem is. This excuse certainly sparks the body into being sick so we will not have to deal with a job or be where we feel out of place and miserable.

"Energy will stay within the body unless you consciously let it go."

Sounds just like ghost energy, does it not?

"Are you now ready to release this energy that may not be for your Highest Good?"

Understanding The Past

If a client insists on me telling them about their past lives, I explain that it is important to stay in the now and work out what is going on in this lifetime. Only when I am not able to locate a specific reason for their problems in this life, do I search out and bring back information from the past. Our past helps us to understand and heal, only if we are willing to let it go. Work with your Guides first, then if you are still not clear, seek out a Lightworker.

There is a great Universal design in the Astral Plane, waiting to connect with us in spite of our 'free will and ego.' With our negative past behind us, we are free to float easily on the wings of Angels into the future.

Most of my adult life I wondered why I was here; I felt I was just wasting time and space. I would often say to God, "Use me or loose me!" These feelings occasionally still arise. Sometimes when I am part of a conference, show or Expo, and there is not much traffic or I am sitting around waiting for people to seek me out, I will ask, "Why am I here?" There have been times when I have lectured to an audience of three. At the end of every show, the reason for my existence always reveals itself. If I connect with one or a dozen ready and willing souls guided to me for help, I know there was a purpose for my being there. I love who I am and I love what I do because,

"Love, is the driving force of the Soul"

Many groups incarnate at the same time. Their energies are so similar that no matter what part of the world you live, when you feel that special soul spark, you will recognize them as your helpful soul-mates, even if you are not sure why you are feeling that connection.

I believe we have been all races and genders during our past lives, and will reunite with a family member or one we were married to. If you feel stirrings of intimacy toward someone of the same sex, it was probably because you were married or lovers in a former life. One possible reason for this type of rekindling is to help work out unresolved issues with the one who once loved you and loves you still, even if they happen to be the same sex.

My remembrance of someone

I met Jane Davis, who lives in California, at an Expo in Dallas. Our booths were right next to each other. Jane was preparing Green Magic smoothies containing 17 food products which I was drawn to drink. Throughout the convention I felt a close bond with Jane. At the end of the convention, she told me that the turnout had been poor, but she felt she came to Dallas just to meet me.

The trip was not a total loss (they never are)

The same weekend, I taught a class on the use of gemstones as healing tools, at three Whole Foods Supermarkets. At one of the stores, I was not paying attention and left my jewelry case under a wagon and it was stolen. I asked myself, "Could the belief that I am protected when I work be flawed?" I was guided to remember that when I first carried my jewelry case into the convention center, I made the statement, "God, this bag is heavy; I wish my load was lighter!" Now I understood, to some degree, *I had asked for what happened*. The underlying lesson I was starting to understand was,

"Even in adversity a Light comes forth to show you the way."

I returned home the following Monday. Early that evening I received a call from the police detective who was handling the case. He told me that most of my jewelry had been recovered. He also said that an 18 year old, part-time employee, took the case when he saw it under the wagon. I had made friends with one young associate manager there who worked hard in helping me search the store. He was the one who discovered who took my jewelry. He told the detective that he saw this young man wearing a crystal cross in the store, and he *just knew* it was one of my special pieces. The detective asked me if I wanted to prosecute the boy for stealing. I told him, "No, karma will get him, and I don't mean Miranda." He said he understood and would ship what was left of my property back to me.

I feel this boy and I had a past connection. There are always unresolved "do unto others as you would have them do unto you" at work, in the 'karmic all knowing realm.' It is possible this boy may have done a good turn for me, or I stole from him in another life and since I was in his proximity, it was time for me to return the favor for our karma to come full circle. Anything is possible with Universal interventions.

All in all, the trip was filled with karmic twists just waiting to be mended or made aware of. Meeting Jane helped me to make the decision to return to teaching about nutrition and food supplements, as I did when I worked in health food stores. I had also been asking for something more to do, other than just working with gemstones and minerals, long before that trip. The loss of my merchandise was a wake up call that I took to mean, *material objects are not necessary to do my work.* This was confirmed when I got the messages, "Have hands and mind will travel; always do everything for love and the money will come."

"Whenever anything happens, no matter how small, large or devastating, it all happens for a reason."

CHAPTER 6

Attunement Stories

Seeing color in a different light

Most of my clients come to me unable to discover, on their own, the underlying causes of their emotional and physical difficulties. With Sweet Spirit's Guidance, I tune-in and learn what they need to know. I use many techniques, one of which is explaining how colors can help them understand the underlying truths that will set them free.

During initial work-ups with clients, I ask "What color or colors do you refuse to wear or have a problem with?" I use this question to find out if there are any conflicting reasons why they have chosen not to wear a certain color. Their answers are always quite interesting, since colors signify what is going on in your present and past emotional state.

One day I was working with art students and I noticed three girls wearing black. One completely wore black. After class, I asked her why, even though she works with color in her art work she chose to only wear black. Her answer amazed me. She said that lately she had not felt like getting up to come to class, let alone taking the time to chose a color coordinated outfit. I delved further by asking what was going on in her life before she started to feel this way. She told me her mother was forcing her to take art classes when she really wanted to take classes in creative writing. This student's explanation told me that by wearing only black, she was hiding her anger towards her mother behind her colorless emotion. Since color was what she was forced to work with, color is what she chose to be devoid of.

I have found in my studies that the colors and their traits have both a negative and positive connection on body/mind reaction.

Orange and yellow are the colors that most chose not to wear. When I asked why, their answers warranted further investigating. The reasons why are...

- **Orange:** Emotional self. Negative: *Pain.* Positive; *Cour- age and happiness.* Orange removes inhibitions. When you get out of your pain you get into your courage.
- **Yellow:** Mental self. Negative: *Fear.* Positive: *Power, wis- dom, increases self-esteem.* Release your fear and create be- ing in your own power.

Other colors and their emotional meanings and affirmations:

- **Red:** Physical self. Negative: *Rage.* Positive: *Increases vi- tality, leaders.* I am open and motivated to be all I can be.
- **Green and pink:** Unconditional love of self. Negative: *Envy, jealousy, disorganized.* Positive: *Giving, balance and healing.* I embrace and love all my emotions.
- **Blue:** Thinking self. Negative: *Sadness.* Positive: *Commu- nication, knowledge.* I tell people how I really feel and what I want and need from them.
- **Indigo or Navy Blue:** Unconscious self. Negative: *Wishy- washy, a daydreamer.* Positive: *Intuitive and understand- ing.* I go within to find my answers.
- **Purple:** Spiritual self. Negative: *Too grounded, not opening to your Higher Self.* Positive: *Creative, humanitarian.* I am fully open and aware of all my Guides and Angels in The Universal Realm.
- **Black:** Altered self. Negative: *Invisibility or protection.* Posi- tive: *Safety,* as in protecting yourself or feelings of, *Why am I afraid to stand out? Who or what am I hiding from?* I no longer fear the unknown.

Personally, I have never felt drawn to wear black, mainly be- cause it is a color void of light. I feel vibrant when I wear a variety of colors covering the spectrum of the rainbow.

* * * * *

A client once told me that she refused to wear baby blue. One day as we were walking through the lingerie department of Neiman Marcus, I noticed a *baby blue* robe on the rack. At that moment I received the message, "Touch her arm with the robe." When I did, her face turned white and she looked like she was going to faint. I caught her and reacting instinctively said, "You're there! Tell me what you see and feel!" In a childlike voice she whispered, "I see my mother with her ugly red hair. She's in a coffin covered with a *baby blue shroud.*"

She was angry with her mother for abandoning her when she was 12. Remember that she mentioned her mother's "ugly red hair?" Strangely enough, my client wore red every time I saw her, which meant that she was able to outwardly express her anger and feelings of abandonment. By refusing to wear baby blue (communication) she was stuffing her rage (red). This was keeping my client stuck in a relentless anger towards her mother that continued well past her death. When she came to visit me the next day, I noticed her whole demeanor was remarkably changed; she proudly wore *a baby blue dress!*

* * * * *

A friend once told me she hated olive green and refused to wear it. I asked when did she first notice her dislike for that color. She took a deep breath thought about what I said, and started to cry. She told me she had been attacked and raped by a man wearing an olive green jacket. Instead of getting help dealing with this, she chose to blame the color, blocking out the face of the attacker. That particular color then became offensive to her whenever she came in contact with it.

When I explained the color theory, she realized that it was not the color but the man she hated. Denying the rape only served to keep her anger alive and continuously affected her life. With this awareness, she finally released the physical and emotional abuse that she chose to push down into the reaches of her subconscious *hoping* it would disappear. This is what Benjamin Franklin said about hope, "He that lives on hope will die fasting."

These stuffed feelings had been hidden behind the color, so to speak, because the real issue, the rape, was too much for her to accept and deal with.

"We bring into our life that which we fear the most."

I have asked clients who have been raped, "Have you ever feared being raped before it happened?" Each time their answer was a resounding *yes*. They had feared being raped most of their lives.

Whenever you look at colors or anything that you dislike in tensely, you must go within and allow all your misplaced anger to surface. It is important to understand why you are feeling that way. After you go within, ask your Higher Self, "What is my issue with this color?" or any other on-going issue you wish to release. Allow yourself to re-connect with the first time the feelings or incident appeared. Now ask for help to understand the true reasons for these feelings. Let your mind bring up all the secret feelings that are hidden; to be processed and released.

> *"Your subconscious is the hidden,*
> *closeted storehouse to all your secrets."*

I have uncovered that it is not what we think that creates our problems. The emotional disturbances left unchecked and hidden from our conscious grasp, will have a lasting effect on our emotional body.

* * * * *

While I was attending a Conference held in Las Vegas, I noticed in the lobby of the hotel a tall lovely woman with long blond hair, walking toward me with the aid of a walking stick. After the introductions, she said she was also participating in the conference. I asked her if she would prefer to get through the conference without the use of her stick and she quickly answered, "Of course I would!"

We went up to my room and I proceeded to ask the leading questions that my Guides always supply me with, in order to efficiently find the reasons for my clients' problems. She told me she was a belly dancer and had a boyfriend who did not appreciate what she considered her career. Instead, he chose to judge what she enjoyed doing as a form of exhibitionism; driving him to extreme bouts of jealousy. Being the dutiful girlfriend, she wanted to please him although it meant giving up a career she loved. In order to solve her problem in a way she could live with and keep her boyfriend happy, she *emotionally* created her *physical* ailment. What a dilemma! One she found herself in, whenever she gave up control of her life to another.

Unfortunately, in her case, her emotional dis-ease manifested itself in her legs. I helped her to understand how the emotional part of her brain sent a signal to her body, creating her obvious physical ailment.

"No one can hurt you without your permission!"

When she understood how she had emotionally and mentally caused her dis-ease — the pain in her legs — she chose to resolve this situation by releasing the boyfriend who was always disapproving and controlling. With that decision, she got up from the bed and walked through the remainder of the conference unencumbered.

"If you feel you are being hurt or taken advantage of in any way, immediately take back your power and put an end to their control!"

When you are willing to be controlled and can not refuse the other person anything because you fear that they will leave you, even if what they ask is abhorrent to you they usually end up leaving anyway. Or you finally get to the point when you have had enough and leave them. Uncontrollable behavior brings about **fear** (an acronym for "False Evidence Appearing Real") and creates the belief that somehow your existence, wishes and desires need validation from an outside source other than yourself.

When you go within and discover the true causes of all your unhealthy beliefs, you will quickly remove the negative energy that keeps you from moving towards the next level of self love and freedom.

CHAPTER 7

Traveling Stories from Outside the Country

Whenever I travel, I always ask my Guides, "What do you want me to do? Where do you want me to go next?" Including, "Where do you want me to eat?"

When Mom made her transition in 1988, she left me a sum of money that I chose to use on a dream escape to England, Scotland, Ireland and Wales. I strongly feel that I have had many past lives in that part of the world and recognizing them is another way to experience a connection to my "Wholeness."

In the 1980's, I was in a British theatrical production in Houston. I particularly enjoy doing British productions, because mimicking an English accent comes naturally to me. (Past lives come in handy!) At the time, I was working at a Ramada Inn. During a lunch-break, I was going over my lines when I overheard a woman talking with a British accent. I walked over to her and said, "I'm studying to appear in a British farce called, "Key for Two," that takes place in Brighton; would you mind demonstrating what a Brighton accent sounds like?" She just laughed and said, "Since you live in Texas, I don't think it really matters. All you need do to be effective, luv, is to throw in a smattering of 'shants' and 'chants.'" I laughed with pure delight at her candor and humor and that day she and I made a soul connection. Before she rushed off, we exchanged names and addresses, and I found out that this charming lady, Ann, was also an actress and a schoolteacher in Yorkshire, England.

A year later when I was ready to plan my dream escape, I wrote to Ann and told her I was coming to Great Britain. She answered my letter immediately and wrote, "Jolly good. Let me know when you are coming and I'll make arrangements for you to stay with my husband Jeffrey and me and some of my friends and relatives." Before I left, I had asked Ann, "What can I bring you as a memento of Houston?" She told me she would like a picture of Houston's beautiful downtown skyline, which she said she only glanced at on her way to the airport. I happened to be working with a photographer that week, so I asked him if he had any recent pictures of downtown. He told me that only days before he had taken some and he would be honored to give me a large framed print, that I could take to England for my friend.

I arrived at Heathrow Airport and Ann's sister, Margaret, was waiting for me at the gate. Before we took the train to her home, I told her that I had to use the ladies room or as the English so quaintly phrase it, "I'm going to spend a penny." When I entered the wash room, I noticed a gate and a box where the 'penny' had to be placed before you had access to the facility. I must have looked alarmed because the attendant came over and asked, "What's wrong, dearie? You look positively glum." I told her, "I don't have any British coins because I just got here from the States." At first I felt she was giving me 'such a look' that suggested, "Dumb Yank!" (or Damn Yankie!) But that look quickly turned into a sweet smile of understanding when she said, "Not to worry, luv, just slip under the gate — the first one's on me!" Sporting another big smile she said, "Welcome back to England" and *winked!* Covered in chill bumps, I thanked her for being so kind, and slipped under the gate.

We took the train to Margaret's stop and picked up her car for the twenty minute drive from the railroad station. In the car, she told me that Ann would be coming for me early in the morning for the drive to her home in South Yorkshire. Ann arrived at her sister's home bright and early, and I was so happy to see her again.

The first leg of the trip went easy and effortlessly, just the way I like it. I stayed with Ann and her college professor husband, Jeffrey, for five days. They lived in a comfortable, typical English country home, with a spacious warm kitchen, a well manicured garden, and a huge bathroom with a large roomy bathtub; the kind with the big lion paw legs. During my entire visit with Ann, my whole body languished in 'big tub heaven.'

Bert, Ann's cousin, unexpectedly arrived during my visit. He sold small folding bicycles that fit perfectly in the boot (trunk) of the car, and were mostly used for short countryside cycling. He was quite an enjoyable fellow, so when he asked if I would like to accompany him to the IMAX in downtown Yorkshire, I agreed.

I took many pictures of the town and its people and got to see my first IMAX movie. I remember being compelled to take one picture in particular at the IMAX; it was a photo of an elderly, toothless man, sitting in the lobby of the theater. Alone on a bench, sound asleep; his head bowed down almost to his knees. When the old gentleman's picture was processed it looked good enough for the cover of a magazine

After my five day staying with Ann and Jeffrey, we drove to York, a large city in Yorkshire, to stay with their friends for the night. The next day, we took in some local color, and visited a pub on the way back. When it came time to order, Ann asked if I would like some lemonade. I answered yes but when it arrived, I was surprised to see that England's version of lemonade was '7-up.' I also had my first "Shandy" drink; black beer laced with 7-up. It was quite good, considering I am not partial to beer. After the pub, we visited the Bowes Museum containing a large variety of Renaissance paintings and antiquities. Next, we went to Stratford-on-Avon and walked the same streets as William Shakespeare. I also stood outside his house and read a brass plaque that more or less stated when he had lived and wrote there. The full day ended with a trip to see a play at the famous King George Theater, still well maintained and continuing to look the same when Royalty and the common folk of that era came to hear the works of Shakespeare, Mallory and many others. Being in this theater and sitting on the same hard wood seats used hundreds of years ago, I felt that I was back in time, *once again spending a penny or a tuppence,* to see a play. Or could I have been one of the male per-formers? Wondering, "To be or not to be, that is the question." So what was the answer? I wonder if I found any back then. Sitting and watching the play, I could sense the energy from the past swirling throughout the halls as it brought on yet another case of 'the chill bumps,' this time caused by remembering. All I know is that once again it felt good to be surrounded by that 'old thespian gang of mine.'

We arrived back at Ann and Jeffrey's home that evening and the following morning, they drove me to the train station where I left for my next stop — Edinburgh, Scotland.

I went to Scotland to recognize and bless each coincidence that crossed my path, and with another assignment.

A friend's Scottish mother asked me to pick her up something from her homeland; something she could hold and 'feel' like she was home. I had no idea what that could be, so I gave it up to The Universe and proceeded with the trip. (When in doubt surrender, give it up and let it go.)

I stayed at a Bed & Breakfast, which was the result of yet another coincidence. *The coincidences flowed non-stop.* When I was at a bookstore in Houston, a travel book literally fell into my hands from the shelf. Inside *The Frommer's Travel Book*, I found the name of this particular B & B, and decided to book a reservation sight unseen.

When I arrived at the train station, the manager of the B & B was waiting to pick me up, which he claimed was not company policy, but I knew he had been guided to pick me up anyway. This was a definite confirmation for buying the book. An extra benefit to staying at this B & B was meeting the manager's son who *was an actor* appearing in a play at the local playhouse a few miles up the road. I thought it would be a Scottish play, being in Scotland, but the show took place in New York. When the play was finished, I went backstage to talk with the performers and acknowledged them on how authentic their New York accents sounded.

My original plan was to stay in Edinburgh for three days and Glasgow for two, but I was having so much fun in Edinburgh, I stayed there the entire five days. During the day, I would walk the three miles to town where I found a marvelous spacious park. This was a popular meeting place for golfers, students, visitors and vendors, all taking the time to commune with the natural beauty of the land given to their townsfolk. In the park, I met people from all over the world and we exchanged philosophies. Some days, while leaning against the side of a long grassy incline, I meditated, soaking up the sun's rays, as they pierced the dense rows of trees while waiting for *what would come next.*

Although I was loving my sojourn in Edinburgh, I was missing one thing. I love eating healthy natural foods. As delicious as the Scottish dishes are, I began longing for a crisp vegetarian meal. One day, on one of my walks, I found myself being guided down a small alley parallel to the main road I usually took to town. I walked with the 'celestial feeling' of my Guides being with me, when I found three buildings all containing what I had been craving.

I chose one that looked the most like it would serve vegetarian dishes and walked in. I sat at the first table facing a large window overlooking the cobblestone courtyard. Suddenly, I felt someone staring at me. I turned to see a handsome, long dark-haired young man in his mid-20's, sitting at the table directly behind me. I said hello and introduced myself. I explained that I was touring Great Britain in search of adventure. He said his name was Christopher and he was a history student and would be honored to show me the historical sights of his birthplace. Since this was a guided meeting I felt comfortable enough to be escorted by Chris.

He showed me building after building displaying brass plaques with the names of famous writers or poets and the year they lived or worked there. The homes, considering they were hundreds of years old, were in excellent condition. In the evenings, he escorted me to night-spots and coffeehouses to satisfy my love of dancing and people-watching. Walking on the ancient cobblestone streets, I felt I was once again in the past and loving every minute of it.

As I prepared to leave for Ireland, I remembered the request asking me to bring back that special something from my friend's mother's homeland. I thought about her request for several days but nothing really jumped out at me. (So I thought!) On the way back from my last visit to the park, I passed a small round rock that sat right in the center of the sidewalk that had caught my interest daily. Since this rock remained in the same place every day, I concluded this rock wanted to come back with me. I picked it up and it felt wonderful to hold. Later, when I returned to the United States and placed the stone in the woman's hand, she closed her eyes and said, "Yes!" I knew that once again, The Universe had guided me and I had responded appropriately.

There are also those coincidences that are warning signs. Recognizing and blessing them is still important, since they help us make choices. When we make the right choices, Universal signs become even more dramatic, as in what happened in Ireland.

My next destination was Dublin where I stayed with a woman, Mary, and her son, Michael, that I found through a friend who had traveled to Ireland the year before. My friend had given me their address so I wrote asking Michael if he knew of a place where I could stay. In his letter, Michael said he was staying with his mother until he found his own place, but there was an extra room if I wanted to stay with them. I accepted, feeling comforted knowing his mother would be there.

Michael picked me up at the ferry and it was not ten minutes into the trip when we had a flat tire. "But not to worry," my new friend announced. I'm thinking, why? Was it because the tire deflated right in front of a Pub? — the emotional act of not moving on or being stuck.

Looking back, this was an awakening and warning of things to come, and I wished I had heeded this subtle message from The Universe.

After I had gone to bed that night, I was awakened by men yelling outside my window. They were loud and obviously drunk. Mary came into the room apologizing profusely, "Please excuse my people." It seems that Sunday, Ireland had won their first football match over England in over 200 years. Outside I heard men shouting, "F—k the British," over and over. Finally, the police came and hauled the group away.

The next morning, Michael offered to show me the sights of southern Ireland. Our first stop was Dublin's Parliament building, equivalent to our White House, because I had an appointment to meet with Prime Minister Charles Haughey. Officially, I was acting as a courier for a magazine that was interviewing political officials on the hobbies people in power enjoyed and I carried two letters of intent; one for Prime Minister Charles Haughey and one to Prime Minister Margaret Thatcher of England.

I was sitting in the waiting room for my meeting, when a man approached me and introduced himself as the Secretary to the Secretary's Secretary to the Prime Minister. He apologized and explained that the Minister was not able to see me personally but he assured me that the letter would be delivered. I asked him if someone could take a picture of us holding the document as proof that I was here, since I was not going to personally deliver it. He agreed.

I found out from the Secretary that I was sitting on the same hard wooden bench as the French Prime Minister, also waiting to meet with Prime Minister Haughey. I was certainly doing some fancy mingling that day!

After Michael and I had lunch, we took off for a city that was 30 miles away that he wanted to show me. I had no idea that a trip over 30 miles in Ireland is considered a day trip. There are no elaborate highways as in the States. Great Britain's highways are known as motor ways, consisting of two lanes similar to our streets. I did not find out until well into the trip, that he had decided we were going to stay together overnight in a hotel. I was extremely uncomfortable with what felt like an underhanded plan, and although I knew I could take care of myself, I was not prepared for an overnight outing.

By now, I was intuitively feeling that this man was not to be trusted.

On the road, we picked up two female French hitchhikers. Michael immediately began flirting with both of them, and invited them to stay with us at the hotel. Unexpectedly, he stopped in a small village. He slipped out of the car, not inviting anyone to go with him, and told us he would be back soon. His departure definitely did not feel kosher. About 30 minutes later, I started to feel anxious and told the two hitchhikers that I was going to look for him. I found him at, what else? A Pub. I peeked inside and saw him with another woman. (Talk about having a 'woman in every port!' This guy could give sailors a run for their libidos!) I walked back to the car and described the scene to the girls, who decided this man's games were too much for them. They bade me farewell and good luck and walked up the block looking for their next ride.

When Michael returned, I told him to continue his trip alone because I did not appreciate his blatant shenanigans. I told him I would take the bus back to his mother's. So, 'it shouldn't be a total loss,' I told him that before he continued on his trip, I wanted him to find me a hotel for the night. At least he did not have a problem with my request, and took me to a lovely inn with a flowered courtyard, and left.

My day had been frustrating, and potentially frightening. After getting settled, I decided to do what I always do; go within, relax and receive guidance. Afterwards, I had an early dinner with an unusual two glasses of wine at a nearby restaurant; walked back to my room and passed into a peaceful sleep. The next morning I took a long walk around the village. At exactly 11:00 a.m., the watch Mom left me suddenly stopped. That was odd, because I had the old battery replaced before I left on my trip! I took the watch to a jeweler who could not find anything mechanically wrong. When I placed it back on my wrist, *it started working*! I realized I was being sent a message. I started thinking back over everything that happened. I know the number 11 in numerology is a sacred Master Number, and it was my Mom's watch. Why would it stop in Ireland, and not in England or Scotland? I was starting to get the feeling that it might have been Mom's way of saying 'hello' and that she was with me in 'spirit' when she felt I needed her the most.

I safely returned the next day to Mary's house by bus. Looking at me perplexed, she asked me what happened to her son. I did not want to tell her what really happened and what I thought of her son. She was a sweet lady and I am sure she knew what kind of a man he was, I told her we just had a parting of the ways because I wanted to stay longer in the quaint village we had lunch in.

With my visit completed in Ireland, I took a cab to the ferry and started on the return trip to England. There I caught a bus to Wales and stayed with another of Ann's friends, Paula, a geriatric nurse. One evening, I felt guided to show her how to use foot reflexology, a wonderful healing massage that works on the meridians that links all the organs and body. She agreed to learn because she felt it would be beneficial to use on her patients. I taught her this procedure on her living room couch, while her family curiously watched. She later wrote how great her patients felt when she applied this ancient form of healing.

Paula's family lived near a 200,000 year old slate mountain. On top of the mountain I saw what appeared to be the face of an old man with a long chin and nose, probably carved by nature. Paula's husband informed me that none of the townspeople knew how the head got there; it just appeared one day! The stone outline reminded me of the old man on the bench I had taken a picture of at the IMAX in Yorkshire! Could it be, *The face of an ancient Angel?*

During our walk around the mountain, I picked up a piece of slate, large enough for the entire family of four to scratch their names on. Having all their names written indelibly on a piece of history was my favorite souvenir of the trip.

One day during my stay in Wales, Paula took me to an ancient historic castle. While at the castle, I was drawn to place my hands on one of the cold bare walls. I felt tremendous sadness and quickly removed my hand. Next, we walked up the stone steps that wound around the entire castle to the top. Suddenly, I received the message to take a picture through a window that was only a square hole in the wall, looking outward to nothing but sky. I did as I was asked and took the picture. When it was developed I saw a white apparition on the left side of the window that looked like it was floating. If I had to guess what happened I would venture to say it was a wee ghosty that communicated to me to take its picture. *I wonder if we knew each other in another life?*

After the trip to Wales, I decided to take the bus to Bath, England. As I waited for the bus to arrive I had to *spend another penny*. This time I had the penny to spend. When I was coming back up the stairs after using the facilities, I overheard a woman pleading with the attendant to let her through even though she did not have the penny (sound familiar?) only this woman was not as nice as my Angel attendant. I handed the troubled young woman a penny and said, "This one's on me. I truly understand how you feel," and walked to the terminal store to buy some goodies for the trip. When I got on the bus, I saw the woman I had helped, and took this as a sign to walk over and meet her. I asked her if the seat next to her was taken and it was not. We struck up a conversation and she told me her name was Diane and she was from Canada; like me she was traveling alone through Great Britain. We connected immediately so I asked her if she had a hotel to stay in when she arrived in Bath. She said that she did not. I heard those familiar intuitive wheels turning, so I told her I had a reservation at a B & B and asked her if she would be interested in sharing expenses. She happily agreed. When we arrived, the owner gave us a larger room. As a result of sharing a room, it cost less than if we had roomed separately; all because of our chance meeting. (Yeah right!) With the money we saved, we were able to see more of the sights, including the Roman baths. At the Baths, you are not permitted to sit on the railing, but the rebel within us took over and we did just that, as a smirking Julius Caesar watched us in the background. Afterwards we went to a pub and laughed about our escapades of the day, 'til the wee hours of the morning.

On the last day, we lounged around the pool while the rays of the first sunny day warmed us, sharing stories about our lives. She told me her father had died only a few weeks prior, and she had decided to take this trip alone to work through her grief. I shared with her that my mother had died a few weeks ago too. With the sharing of this information, we now understood the true reason for our meeting. We hugged and cried, releasing our much needed bottled-up emotions. I would venture to guess that both our parents were probably jumping for joy during our mutual cleansing fest.

Later that day, Diane walked me to the bus station for my trip back to London; she would be going on to Stonehenge. I wanted to go with her, but Ann's sister was expecting me .

Since I could not visit Stonehenge, Diane was kind enough to send me some wonderful pictures when she returned to Canada.

London was the last leg of my tour

I arrived in London on Sunday by train. I had only one day to explore London town because Ann's sister, Margaret, was meeting me later that evening at the train stop by her house. Leaving the station, I turned right and following my guidance found a wonderful museum. I walked up the museum's white marble steps, and saw a sign that read, "Russian Paintings donated for Exhibition" and it happened to be the last day of the showing. I walked past corridors that held walls and walls of magnificent paintings. I was so overwhelmed by so much beauty at one time, from an era that must have been bringing up too many of my past lives at once, that I ran from the museum on unsteady legs, and sat on the steps until whatever had come over me passed.

When I calmed down, I continued on my walk, heading towards Downing Street so I could deliver the letter to Mrs. Thatcher from the magazine that was compiling data about her hobbies. When I arrived, I found two Bobbies or English C.O.P.S — Constable On Patrol (now you know where we got the slang term for our police officers.) These fellows were guarding a small gate, which, when lifted, brought you into the courtyard of 10 Downing Street, the headquarters of the Prime Minister. In the past, B.T. (before terrorism) tourists were free to browse around the grounds, as we have guided tours in the White House. I explained to the guards that I had a letter to deliver to Mrs. Thatcher, which had already been authorized by her secretary. At first I was blatantly refused. I asked if they would check with her secretary before dismissing me, since I had come all the way from the States. One guard gave in and used his walkie-talkie to call his superior for advise. I could tell by his facial expression that I was not going to get past them. So, as I had done at Dublin's Parliament, I asked one guard if he would have his partner take a picture of us holding the letter. They agreed and assured me that the letter would be taken to the Prime Minister's Secretary. I thanked them and continued on to whatever my Guides had in store for me.

I found myself walking through a park, that seemed as big as Washington Square Park in Greenwich Village. At the edge of the park I found a road leading to a big market square where I watched musicians and minstrels perform for tips, similar to those in Washington Square Park on Sundays. I was sitting on a bench watching the sights when all of a sudden I felt something warm and wet hit the back of the collar of my new, expensive brand-named suit that I bought for my meeting with Mrs. Thatcher. I looked up to see a line of pigeons sitting on a telephone line and one was flying off. Without looking at my collar I just knew I had been 'pooped upon.' I also noticed no one else had been 'bombed.' I said to the people staring at me with their Cheshire cat smiles, "Out of all the people in this square, how did that pigeon know I was a Yankee?" One lady called out, "Not to worry; it's good luck." to which we all had a good laugh.

After all that merriment, I continued walking towards the theater and shopping district, similar to Times Square in Manhattan. I happened upon a metaphysical bookstore, an oasis in the desert to me. I entered and was greeted by a likable, smiling young man in his late 20's. I told him I was visiting and only had this one evening to spend in London. He said, "I'll ring up some friends, and we'll all go out to dinner in Soho." I had planned on visiting Soho since I heard it was as touristy as Greenwich Village, but had not found it on my walk through town.

We went to a Japanese restaurant because I told them I liked Sake rice wine. We ate and shared many toasts and I was soon becoming fried! We were having such a great time and I did not want to leave my new London friends, but I had made arrangements to meet Margaret at a specific time at her train stop. Every time I told my dinner companions I had to leave to catch the train, they just laughed and poured me another drink. Finally I said goodbye and wobbled into the street yelling for a taxi. Before I even finished saying the word "taxi," one of those big black Hackney cabs, the one's London is so famous for, came screeching to a stop at my feet. I got in and slurred, "The train — I'm going to be late!" Again, before I finished my words or was able to sit down, the cab sped off in a cloud of diesel smoke. And I thought New York cabs were fast! The driver screeched to a stop in front of the train station in what felt like seconds, for a five mile trip. I tipped him well and ran panting the whole way to the train. I could make out in the blurry distance that the conductor was just about to close the door, which meant the train would be starting *without me*! So I yelled, in typical Yankee fashion, "Don't you dare leave without me!" He graciously held the door wide open until I got there. I thanked him, *he tipped his hat and winked*, and I flopped into my seat.

By now I was getting the message that winking is an Angelic sign!

I told the lady next to me where I needed to stop and asked her to please let me know when we arrived. I then slumped into a take-me-away-for-awhile meditative pose. By the time we got to my destination, Margaret was waiting for me and I had sobered up (what a good meditation will do) When I told her what a great time I had in the city, she said that if I had called her she would have picked me up on a later train. I thanked her for her kindness but told her it was the perfect time to end, "A beautiful day in London town."

Traveling Back In 'The Good Ole U.S. of A.'

While on a trip to San Diego, I received a message to walk up the road. I had been walking for about three miles when I came across a diner. It was breakfast time, so I felt this was where I was being led. While I was eating, I noticed in the booth to my left, two elderly women and a young boy. I felt the boy was the reason I was there. When I finished, I walked over to their table and explained that I was in San Diego teaching about alternative healing modalities. One of the women was interested in learning more from me and asked if I would come to her home and work with her 12 year old grandson, Jason, who had been born with Cerebral Palsy. (I know personally there is something special about being ready for initiation into The Universal Realm at the age of 12).

After arriving at her home, I talked with Jason and decided to perform a "Complete Body Alignment on him. At the end of the session, I explained to the young man that there was an energy source within him that was causing his ailment. I explained, without getting too "woo-woo" for him to understand, that this negative energy would work its way out. I also told him that when he truly understood the lesson he was brought here to complete, he would find peace within his body, mind and spirit.

* * * * *

On another journey, I was guided to yet another restaurant also in San Diego. (What is it with my Guides and food? No wonder I gain weight when I travel!) This spiritually directed meeting ended up being five miles away. I had walked about four when I became so exhausted that I felt I could no longer go another step. I shouted within, "That's it, I'm turning around. I'm too tired to walk any further and my knee is killing me — I need help now!" In an instant, I felt I was being placed on the wings of angels, and glided painlessly to my destination.

I arrived at the restaurant, sat at the counter and ordered breakfast. On the way to the washroom, I noticed three women deeply engrossed in conversation. One of the women stopped in mid-sentence, turned to look at me, then at the gemstone necklace around my neck and she said, "I'm not sure why, but I must talk with you!" I pointed to my stool and suggested she meet me there. When I returned, she was waiting for me. I explained that I was in town teaching how to use stones as healing tools. After breakfast, she drove me back to my hotel to look at my inventory. (Whenever I am asked to walk to a destination, the ride back is always provided.)

The woman was drawn to the Herkimer diamond quartz crystals. These perfectly faceted crystal are found only in Herkimer, New York. Herkimers grow inside the matrix of a dolomite calcium rock surrounded by crystallized druzy which supports it like a baby protected by the placenta in a mothers' womb, unlike quartz rock crystal which grows in red clay. Herkimers can help you to see more clearly, amplify energy and balances your five subtle bodies which consist of mental, physical, spiritual, emotional and etheric. *I never leave home without one.*

During our time together, she shared with me that she lives in Washington, D.C., but felt drawn to return to sunny San Diego. She told me she was in town looking to rent a house, but had not found one yet. She said she happily chose to spend some of the designated 'rent money' on these beautiful gifts to herself. When we completed our transaction, I received an intuitive message about a house for her to rent which I passed on to her. It seems the woman who owned the restaurant where we met was a friend of hers and owned a rent house, but was not happy with the present tenant, therefore, the tenant would be turned out, giving her the opportunity to move in. I asked her what she thought of that. She told me that message felt "*soooo right!*"

* * * * *

During a ten-day county fair in San Jose, California, another exhibitor approached me and started to tell me an unhappy story. I stopped her and suggested making an appointment, so I could give her "delighted attention."

She came back the next day and we sat under a shady tree, as I listened to her tale. When she finished, I said to her, "Make believe I am your Fairy Godmother waving a magic wand and telling you that you can have or do anything you desired with nothing to stop you and if you didn't get paid, would you still do it? Now tell me what would that be?"

"I want to work with seeing-eye dogs and open schools throughout the country, but I don't have the money." She answered.

"Don't think about the money." I explained. "It's more important that you place your intention out into The Universe where your Guides know exactly how to manifest that which is for your Highest Good." I taught her a breathing exercise to help ground her and guided her through a meditation consisting of creating and seeing her hearts' dream in the mind's eye, or third eye located in the middle of the forehead, also known as the frontal eminence during C.B.A. I told her to be explicit about what she asked for, so her message is sent out clearly. For example, you ask for a house and receive it, but do not ask for a way to pay for it, and lose it. When the lesson was completed, we both went back to work at our respective booths. As I walked to my booth, I saw a woman holding a leash to a black Labrador retriever. I looked at my associate, Jane Davis, who, with a puzzled look said, "I felt I had to detain this woman until you returned. Do you have any idea why?" I explained to her that I had just finished a session with a woman who told me she wanted to work with seeing-eye dogs. Jane responded, "That's amazing! I was just chatting with this woman and she told me that she is a dog instructor who also teaches the blind to work with seeing-eye dogs." I began reeling with delight because my client's wish was about to come true within minutes of her request! Turning to the dog trainer I said, "There's a woman you must meet right now!" She agreed to accompany me. We walked across the court to visit the recipient of what could become a wondrous miracle, if she was ready and willing for it to take place. On the way, I let the instructor know I was about to introduce her to a woman who wanted more than anything to work with seeing-eye dogs, and to teach the blind as she did. I approached the unsuspecting woman first, looked into her eyes and said, "Are you ready for your miracle?" When she saw the dog, she appeared confused and teary-eyed. I felt I did my part and it was time to leave these three characters (the dog was also a part of this miracle) alone to complete their Universal Intervention play and to work out the details concerning this woman's future in the realm of, *being in service to the blind.*

This fair lasted a grueling 13 days during a heat wave in a building that got up to 100 degree because it had no air conditioner, but this miracle made it all worthwhile.

Often, I am minding my own business and someone will walk up and tell me about a pain or how miserable their life is, and somehow the words I need to help them comes out in a personal message. I may never see the person again in this life, but in the five minutes we were brought together something profound happens for both of us. I share this with you, because I know that you will experience similar exchanges as you continue on your path. Now, let me tell you more about mine...

Chapter 8

Relationships

Whenever you associate or have a relationship with another person, past emotions in the form of triggers are bound to be called forth. Whether it is something said or an action that brings up feelings and emotions you do not understand, you are being restimulated. We imprint feelings relating to sad memories, thoughts and emotions. Someone comes into our space and brings up those painful memories from the hidden recesses of the mind and we replay those feelings as if they were happening in the moment.

When we first meet someone, we only want to see their good qualities; what they want us to see. We show this side to give a good impression. As relationships progress, we start to mirror *our* faults through *them*. What you do not like about someone is what you do not like about yourself. Some people's idiosyncrasies may seem normal to them but are quite strange to you and visa versa. Sufficed to say, it is not *their* fault that they are restimulating your, oh so, well hidden, unhappy childhood.

For example, you meet someone and their angry controlling behavior is obvious, but you still jump into the relationship believing everything will be fine once they change, because you are going to help them change. Since you have been brought up in that environment, abusive addictive relationships are familiar. Therefore, on some emotional level you tell yourself it must be right even when somewhere in the recesses of your mind you know it will never work. Such a volatile unholy alliance is stimulating to you. If someone who is loving, caring or kind comes into your life you fluff them off. You tell yourself compared to what you are used to, they are too boring or not exciting enough. You also tell yourself you will do your utmost to change the one you are drawn to or change to accommodate them. You are willing to do anything to make it work. How many times have you played that scene out to its same defeating conclusion? Only to blame yourself for another relationship gone awry and wonder what is wrong with you! The only way it has to do with you, is that, instead of healing after the last relationship, you continued onto the next one, thinking there is always someone better just around the corner. The only thing around that corner is *your stuff staring right back at you,* every time you have a problem with those you bring in.

Review each relationship, past and present, and look into the eyes of those you have brought into your life. Let them show you what past emotions you refuse to let go of or you will continue to bring in the same going-no-where relationships; with the same rituals, until you understand why you are making the same mistakes over and over.

These past relationships are your "personal button-pushing emissaries of wisdom" who have not been brought back into your life to continue to make your life miserable as you may think. Nor do they want to be miserable either. It goes both ways in the give-and-take scheme of things. Instead of being angry in their mission to help, thank them for being there to show you how to release the past.

By facing your lions and touching them on the nose, you will find it easier to move on to the next challenge. Everyone knows there is a problem but nobody knows what it is — like being in a sinking boat and *nobody* thought to bring the life jackets!

"Understanding the past is a lifeline to a happier future."

The '*Pains of Growing Up,*' a life play, that leads to the sequel '*The Tell-Tale Life,*' is comprised of parents, siblings, relatives, friends, lovers, spouse, employers and co-workers.

We have choices in the types of relationships we wish to enter into. Some are healthy encounters: positive, empowering, spiritual and physical. These healthy encounters will produce understanding and communication. Unhealthy relationships are those which are negative, controlling and abusive where disharmony and miscommunication thrive.

Unresolved emotions with any or all of your past and present associations will forever evoke disturbances if left unfinished. Learn what you must do to be true to yourself and this will heal the past and help you to move on to your purpose for being.

An empowering relationship is between two or more who feel a soul or heart connection with one another. In other words, these are the souls where your heart feels warm and comfortable in their presence. (Possibly karmic in origin.)

A spiritual relationship is the relationship with your spiritual 'Universal buddies.' The Universe would love you to have a one-on-one relationship with Your Guides and Angels. They are always on call to personally help with life matters when you are not going in the direction you want or when your problems are piling up faster than you can release them by yourself. I find one of the quickest and easiest ways to get in touch with our astral helpers is to meditate or talk to them just before you go to sleep. Ask that your answers come to you upon wakening. Also, use the common phrase, "Give me a sign," and what you need will unfold in the pages of your mind.

Have you ever awakened at 3:00 a.m. for no reason? It could be the kidneys kicking in, wanting your attention (unless you drank water before retiring) asking, "Why haven't you gotten in touch with whatever is 'pissing you off?' If you are ready to know the answer, this is the perfect time to ask us for help."

How about 4:00 a.m.? That is the liver getting your attention, (unless you ate something heavy before sleep) asking, "What's got you stuck and keeping you from moving on? Can we talk?" One woman told me she was awakened at 3:30 a.m. and I told her that she is probably 'pissed off' about being stuck! To which she nodded yes!

I discovered this "Universal-wake-up-call" when I was awakened too many nights for it to be coincidence and I decided to find the cause.

I was told telepathic, spiritual, 'let's talk now' lines are less crowded during the early morning hours. Instead of waking up, turning over and going right back to sleep (if you can!) talk to your willing Guides who want to listen to all that is troubling you. It is less expensive than therapy, and definitely much better than lying wide awake in bed.

Some of my work, as a metaphysical teacher, consists of attending and lecturing at conferences, wellness centers, book stores, psychic health fairs, Whole Food Supermarkets and various other holistic organizations. Many are drawn into my particular space whether I assist with a healing or have a special message just for them from Sweet Spirit. There are usually at least half a dozen or so who will really open their hearts and fully listen to what 'The Higher Universal Intelligence' has to say to them. Usually, the ones who gravitate to me have told me they have traveled between 50 to 200 miles or more, and have no earthly idea why they are standing in front of me. They all say they were brought to me for a reason. These are the ones I definitely know will be open to the information that will be coming through me, for them, whether it is about which crystal would work for them the best; releasing emotional or physical pain or just to receive one of my grand H.U.G.'s (*"Help Us Grow"*).

Physical relationships are the intimate ones or the abusive relationships you unconsciously bring in from unresolved unhappy memories. These are the ones who love to push the buttons that re-stimulate baggage from the past. If allowed, this type of relationship will last until you understand what you must learn from them or until you are ready to be to true to yourself, heal the past and move on to your purpose for being.

"No one really does anything to you. They are your teachers pushing your buttons, from a past not yet resigned."

New relationships cannot begin in your life unless you are willing to make room for them. This is known as "creating a vacuum" and includes cleaning out your closet, home, car, garden or discarding anything old or outdated. If you have not worn a piece of clothing for over six months or have no use for something in your home or office, send it to charity. They will happily relieve you of your unneeded disorder. If you are in the middle of releasing someone from a stormy relationship, you may not want their gifts, photos or clothes hanging around as a reminder of a time best put behind. This includes items left behind after the death of a loved one, when it is time to let go.

"Creating a vacuum helps you to bring in more purposeful people, places and things."

Sexually abusive relationships

Sexual experiences that impacted us as a child, will physically and mentally entice us back as adults. Freud called this "original trauma."

It is extremely important how you react towards situations of this type when dealing with children of impressionable ages.

A young boy and a girl are bathing together and are exploring each other out of curiosity as you walk in on them. Your reaction to what you have just witnessed will create a lasting impression on the children and set the pattern toward how they will relate to their bodies later in life. If you chose to scream and forcibly yank the children out of the tub, your reaction conveys that their actions are intolerable. As adults, they may believe curiosity about the human body is forbidden and deserving of punishment. It also imprints the message that any form of sexual curiosity creates pain or punishment. Talk to them without shaming them; for shame and guilt will follow them throughout their lives. Explain to them curiosity is fine, acting out is not. Remember "Love can move mountains and change mistrust, hostilities and fear."

"Always be prepared to come from love and understanding, no matter what the situation."

My first sexual encounter created a negative experience that followed me into adulthood

When I was about eight, my sister and I went to the local movie theater. After the movie and on the walk home, we heard a man calling us from inside a storefront. He was yelling, "Come over here, little girls, I want to show you something." I was getting a feeling that we better not listen to what he was saying, but my sister let go of my hand and ran over, curious to see what the man had to show us. I ran after my sister to stop her, but it was too late. When I got closer, I heard him say, as he held out his cupped hands, "Would you like to see my surprise? It's in my hands." When he opened his hands, I saw he was holding his penis.

Seeing his penis in that unexpected way, left an indelible impression with me. As a result, I drew into my space several instances when men exposed themselves or masturbated in front of me. This happened four times inside various movie theaters and once when I was lying on a lounge chair at an empty pool at my apartment complex.

The following are stories of (thank God) only near rape situations, which shows the on-going trap I had fallen into

I was at a bar when I met a man who *acted* like a gentleman. It turned out he was a vice-cop. During our conversation, he informed me that when he apprehended rapists, he liked to kick their private parts as hard as he could just to watch them suffer — as he so crudely put it. I suppose that admission should have set off a 'three-alarm warning' to stay away! But I figured if he hated rapists as much as he claimed, I would be safe.

We shared a few drinks and I invited him back to my apartment, where he proceeded to force me, even after I yelled an emphatic NO to his sexual advances. When one says no, it means NO, even if the person forcing you is someone you know; a distinction I found out first hand known as 'date rape.' Thank God he was too drunk to continue and passed out on top of me. I lay there for hours trapped under his heavy body until he woke up around 7:00 a.m. Now he was sober and strong enough to continue his attack on me. By some quick thinking, which has always helped me to diffuse times of trouble in the past, I pointed over to my couch and said to him, "You see that box over there? That's the medicine I'm taking for syphilis, and I'd be more than happy for you to stick it in so it'll eventually fall off." This stopped him in his tracks. He thought about it and said, "Fine, I'll just stick it in your mouth." Deciding that I had had enough of his threats, I found the strength to kick him off me. As he lay on the floor, he gave me a nasty look and got to his feet. When he walked to the door, I yelled, "Just remember, you're no better than those rapists you beat up and arrest for doing exactly what you attempted to do to me."

Since this incident happened in the early 1970s, I did not report it because complaining to the police about a fellow officer got you no where due to an underlying code of brotherhood. I just kept silent, until now!

* * * * *

When I first moved to Houston, I worked as a shoe shine girl. Many of my customers wanted to date me outside work, but I told them that I did not go out with customers. One time I *allowed myself* to be talked into going out to lunch by a handsome smooth-talking fellow. Since I had not brought any 'nut cases' into my life in years, I thought lunch would be safe enough. I also went because I felt it was time to put what I had learned about my sexual addictions to a test!

After lunch, he took me to visit his friend at his place of business, a nearby, area rug store. His friend brought out drinks and pot, but I chose not to join them. While the smooth talking fellow was driving me home, he asked me if I wanted to have some fun in a hot-tub. I clearly refused.

I certainly had not tuned into my intuition the day I agreed to go out with him!

When we arrived at my apartment, he started to walk me to the door which I told him would not be necessary. After I got out of his car, I heard my phone ringing, so I ran inside thankful for a reason to end this farce of a date. In my haste to answer the phone, I forgot to lock the door and he snuck inside. Suddenly I felt a hand on my ankle, and slowly moving up under my dress. I turned and saw him kneeling on the floor. I screamed, "Get out of my apartment or I'll call the police!"

When he left, I thanked The Universe for giving me the strength to put a stop to his unwanted advances and not succumb to my addiction of, 'finding love in all the wrong places.' Nothing like that has happened to me since and that was over nine years ago and counting. These situations showed me that

"There are no secure spaces while you are still

living in an addicted existence."

When I was living in sexual uneasiness, I was sending out some kind of homing signal to others suffering from the same addiction. I had no idea that I was sending such unhealthy vibrations, so I asked The Universe, why? Their reply was,

"Life is unkind to those stuck in the unhappiness from the past."

Only by going within for my answers was I ready and capable of understanding the true nature of my addicted behavior. Unless I healed the past, any future relationships, intimate or otherwise would be bleak.

When these episodes were happening, it seemed as though I was an actor in a play, merely frozen in time, unable to keep myself from watching, but too traumatized to react with the players, all from the too remembered "original trauma."

Sexual Addiction

A man called me to set-up an appointment to see if I could help him understand the reason for a sexual problem he was suffering from. He phoned the next day and explained that he had to cancel the appointment because his lady friend did not want him to seek help. Her own sexual addictions allowed her to believe he had no problem. I asked him what he thought the problem was and he said he had trouble releasing his erections. I suggested having a session on the phone and he agreed.

I guided him to go back to his first sexual encounter. He went all the way back to when he was 12 and on the bed with his mother and her girl friend. He said that he remembered slipping his hand under the covers and secretly fondled his Mom's friend. I asked him to move forward to another time and he shared with me an incident when he traveled to Italy with his school at 15. He said he met an older woman and had his first sexual experience.

Neither of these women put a stop to a behavior that eventually led to his addiction; probably because their sexual triggers were being activated. Therefore, he learned at an early age the powers he possessed — to make women sexually happy.

His sex addictive and women pleasing behavior, started to take over his life until it became physically impossible for him maintain his habit any longer. He finally reached the time in his life when he had to say no more! *Sometimes we only realize there is a problem when our health is at stake!*

"It's okay to say no without hurting people's feelings and it's okay for them to say no to you without hurting your feelings."

Who knows what his life would have been like if his mother's friend had said no, and informed his mother who he said had no idea of what was going on that day. I explained to him, "Your addiction has become a debilitating problem, leading to the detriment of your mental and physical safety. Abstaining is the only road to recovering your freedom and independence from the need to make women happy."

By uncovering the truth during our exploration into his subconscious and learning how his addiction originally started, it truly helped him to understand how, why, and when it all began.

This was the first time I attempted such an in-depth session using the phone and I was amazed at how easily it went. I never received payment, but his willingness to work with me led to successfully discovering his problem and that was reimbursement enough.

CHAPTER 9

Getting Help From The Universe

Getting help from The Universe, your Guides, teachers and all there is, is just a thought, feeling, or belief away. Sometimes a good cry or shout will jog loose the dross that may be keeping you from connecting with them. *Remember, The Outer Realm, because of your God-given free will cannot help you unless you ask.*

This chapter is about ways in which help, advice, suggestions or the answers came to those open, ready and willing.

* * * * *

I was traveling on the access road of Loop 610 in Houston, at about 45 m.p.h. when I noticed the car ahead of me was coming closer and closer. I could not understand why it was not moving with the flow of traffic, until I was almost on top of it! I was about to plow into the back of a stranded car when *something* took hold of the steering wheel. In a flash, my car swerved into the left lane and quickly back to the right lane, completely missing the car. A woman traveling in the left lane saw what happened as I passed right in front of her, barely missing her. She looked at me from the opposite lane as if to ask, "How did you do that?" I shrugged because I knew it was nothing I had done that saved my life. As far as I was concerned, I was on my way to meet that immovable object and possible death before that intervention took place.

Whenever I feel fear coming up, I use this helpful phrase, "I call on the White Light of Christ Energy Protection to surround me, enfold me and cleanse me of all that is less than *Christ Perfection*. So be it. Praise God" and fear instantly dissolves.

* * * * *

Another incident, again while driving, happened on I-45 North while coming back from Galveston. All of a sudden a car came flying over a makeshift island used during road construction. I was so busy looking at the oncoming car, that I had no idea it was about to land on top of me. Within a Universal instant (not a measurable time, it's that fast) I felt a force push my foot down on the gas, allowing my car to soar ahead and leaving the flying car to miss me (but not by much!). I thanked God and watched in the rearview mirror as the car crashed down. It took me about 10 minutes before I fully regained my composure and drove off the highway to call 911.

* * * * *

As I was walking up to the waiting area of the Kansas City, Missouri airport, I heard my name being called. I knew it was not one of my Guides because this time it came from *outside* my head. I looked around and saw a woman rushing toward me. I recognized her from a conference I was part of in Houston. She said, "I was sitting here praying for someone to counsel me about a decision concerning whether I should leave my husband or not. This could not be more perfect; I had no idea it would be someone we both knew."

Had we not met in the waiting area, we would have on the plane; our seats were located *in the same aisle!*

* * * * *

After being guided to a Barnes and Noble in Houston, I met two women who gave me permission to use these two wonderful stories.

The first as told to me by Nancy Davenport:

"I went to Louisiana, running from my problems, when I met Robert with whom I quickly moved in with. A week later, the clock in my Chevy truck stopped working for no apparent reason. I stayed with him about three months when I started to feel uneasy. I realized I had rushed into sharing my life with a man I did not know enough about to warrant such a move. With that insight and the heralding information that came blaring from within; *"Get out of this situation now!"* I gathered all my belongings and drove back home to Texas. The moment I crossed over the border, I felt drawn to look at the clock that had remained still during my unhappy time with Robert. To my amazement, the clock was working once again. Time had been standing still for me until I chose to enter the road leading toward a healthier way of life."

It seems The Universe likes to use time pieces to get our attention as they did with me in Ireland when Mom's watch also stopped!

The second story as told to me by Lucretia Lopez:

"I was 14 years old when I had my first visit from the Spirit Realm, a world I did not believe in. I woke out of a sound sleep and looked at the clock next to my bed which read 2:00 a.m. I stared straight ahead and with my eyes wide open, I watched what appeared to be smoke coming from out of the wall, passing through the room and out a closed window.

The next morning I told my mother and grandmother what I had seen. They both agreed the illusion of the smoke must have been created by a car's headlight streaming through the window. I knew it was not probable; no light of any kind could have possibly come in the way the windows are positioned in the room.

That night, I awoke, looked at the clock's luminous dial and saw it was once again 2:00 a.m. I looked ahead and sure enough the strange smoke appeared, following the same path as the night before.

The next morning I told my mother and grandmother that I watched the smoke again as it sailed through my room, but they still didn't believe me. I asked my grandmother if she would sleep in my room that night and see the smoke if it came back again. She agreed. I woke up, glanced at the clock and saw once more that it was 2:00 a.m. I shook my grandmother awake and sure enough the smoke appeared and Grandma saw it too! Now I had confirmation that what I had repeatedly witnessed, for three consecutive nights, was not my imagination. Grandma told my mother that she also saw the smoke racing through the room just as I had described.

I realized that I wasn't crazy and began to think, what could this smoke be trying to tell me? I had a thought. A week ago to the day the smoke incident began, my other grandmother passed away. It must have been my grandmother communicating a final good-bye because I was not with her when she died. Since then, the smoke has never returned."

"To believe, you need not understand."

A client and her missing niece

Laura, a client, asked me to help her make some sense of the circumstances surrounding the disappearance of her niece and her possible murder.

It seems her husband had received an anonymous call one evening and a man told him he had found their phone number in her niece's phone book. The unknown voice told him the girl was dead. Laura told me she did not know if it had been the police or a friend of her niece who found the book and thought the family should know. The caller also told him they would take care of her remains, and hung up without mentioning where the burial would take place. Three years had passed since that ominous call.

At the beginning of the session, Laura showed me letters her niece sent her before she left home some years ago. She said she could not make sense of the underlying messages she felt certain were contained in her niece's writings and poetry that were signed La Trea. I suggested we do a meditation which would reveal to both of us what was going on with her niece.

I held her hand and we went into a meditation that brought us both to a higher plane for the answers to her questions. When it was completed I was told to ask her, "Why do you believe she is dead? Why do you believe the ones who tell you, 'She is no longer of this Earth?'"

I asked her, "In your heart, do you still feel she is dead and buried?" She looked at me with tears in her eyes and said, "No, I don't feel she is gone!"

With that new awareness, we again read over the letters with the knowledge that this time we were dealing with the living. I held the letters in my hands and received the message, "These are well hidden coded messages that explain how she is dealing with her unholy and tormented life within the satanic world. Although she has physically left, she remains a troubled soul running for her life from the evil ones who still seek her out."

I explained to Laura, "Your best course of action is to surrender all to God. There is danger if you continue your search on a path with the dark forces; an evil beyond your comprehension." I also told her, "When your niece calls on the spiritual strength she needs to break the ties that keep her from "the pure essence of freedom," she will once again be One with the Light, as a free and untroubled child of God."

What I told Laura may not have been what she came to hear, but at least she learned, from our Guides, that *her niece is alive* and she was no longer involved with the cult but in hiding.

This is one of many poems written by La Trea. I reprinted it in my book, because I feel it best describes Laura's niece's emotional pain during her time with the satanic cult; pain we all have felt at one time or another.

Those so inclined please say a prayer, and help bring Laura's niece, La Trea, back to the Light.

Last Step

Are there any reasons
worth this pain I have?
My life is like the seasons;
Winters always been the best I've had.

The last step's always the hardest;
At least that's what they say.
But what could be so hard
If you know you're going the right way.

At times it seems my mind's at war
with ideas of those who are unseen.
I don't know what they're fighting for
and it is invading my life
which is my dream.

So as I'm walking this thin line
that leads back to the real me,
the last step's only the hardest
if you're not sure of what you see,

— La Trea

* * * * *

While at the Vancouver Pacific National Exhibition, a woman named Phyllis told me a story with definite *Spiritual overtones*. She walked into my tent and after talking for a while, we got on the subject of reincarnation. She said that she did not believe in it and became completely still. She said that she felt compelled to share a story with me, one that she had only told her sister, because she believed people would think her crazy. For some reason, Phyllis felt I would understand what she was about to tell me.

She began by telling me about her brother who was killed during WW2, when Canada sent their troops to help the resistance fight and keep Amsterdam from Nazis occupation. She told me she decided to visit her brother's grave somewhere in Holland. I asked her why the government had not sent her brother's body back to Vancouver. She said that during battle, Canadian soldiers were buried where they fell.

Her story continued on a train headed for what she thought was a visit to her brother's grave, but turned into a trip filled with more than she could have expected.

At one stop, she saw a flower market. She remembered her brother loved carnations and wanted to take some to his grave. She got off the train and walked through the entire market but did not find a single carnation. She thought it odd not to find even one amongst the plethora of flowers, but quickly dismissed it. She returned to the train empty-handed and continued on to her destination. A short ways up the track she got the strange feeling that she had to get off at the next station. She walked aimlessly around the station when she noticed a kiosk containing flowers. When she got closer, Phyllis saw that the whole cart was completely filled with carnations in all colors. She told me by now she had the feeling that she was being guided by some unforeseen force. This time, she got back on the train with an armful of her brother's favorite flower and with the strong feeling that she was now ready to complete her trip. While on the train, she asked the conductor to alert her when she arrived at her stop, and settled down to a nap.

Phyllis felt a tap on her shoulder from a woman who said that she noticed all her flowers, and thought she must be going to the cemetery, the next stop on the line. She thanked the woman and wondered why the conductor did not wake her. She said she realized if the woman had not awakened her, she would have missed her stop. Before she left the train, Phyllis turned to say good-bye to the woman when she realized, *there were no other women on the train!* The conductor came up to her on the platform and apologized for not alerting her to her stop. He claimed he had completely forgotten about her request.

When Phyllis finally arrived in the town where the cemetery was, she had no idea where to go from there. She said she thought, "What do I do now?" Phyllis noticed a solitary man sitting on a bench in the deserted train station. As she walked towards him, she realized it was early Sunday and most people were probably home or at church. When she reached the man, she asked him if he knew the way to the Canadian cemetery. He said, "Keep walking south until you see a cross on a hill; there you will find that which you seek." (The usual old English words of a Universal Guide!) She started walking in the direction the man suggested, flowers in hand, for what seemed like hours but still had not seen the cross. Finally she saw a car, the first since she began her quest and flagged it down. She asked the driver where the cemetery was. He said, "Look to the cross for what you seek."

At last, over the next hill, she saw the much talked about cross and headed for it. She had finally found the cemetery. Her next step was to locate her dear brother's grave. She did not see a caretaker, so she read headstone after headstone. Suddenly, out of nowhere, a big gust of wind literally picked her up off the ground, carried her a few feet in the air, and gently positioned her in front of a grave. She looked down at the headstone to nothing less than a miracle — it was her brother's!

Shaking with excitement, she chose one red carnation, his fa-vorite color, and placed it next to a single pansy, his second favor-ite flower growing *only* on his grave. She encircled the two flowers with more carnations and she took the remaining carnations and scattered them between the graves of the other brave souls buried so far from their homeland. With that task of love completed, she realized it was getting late and she had to get back to the train station before it got dark.

On her way back, Phyllis came across a forest that beckoned her in. She said the trees in this forest were growing in a most unusual sequence. As she pondered the strange layout, she once again felt a helpful gust of wind lift her off the ground, and move her deeper into the forest. It placed her down on an unusually large clearing within a dense forest. She just stood there while lov-ing Angelic hands surrounded her, as she began to feel a close connection with her brother.

When she returned to Vancouver, Phyllis told me she did not know if she would tell anyone about the unusual events that had taken place during her trip, where she was etherically able to be with her brother one more time.

I understood, because that is how I felt when my father visited me. She finally decided to tell her sister, the one person she be-lieved would understand. When she got to the part about the strange forest, the large clearing, and the connection she felt with her brother, her sister told her that the clearing was where their brother had been killed! Phyllis's sister never told her this before, but she had taken the same trip and everything Phyllis described also happened to her. After she returned home she asked the gov-ernment about the strange clearing in the forest. They explained to her that they cleared the area where their soldiers had fought and died, as a memorial to them.

When Phyllis finished her chilling story, she looked concerned, so I asked her what she was feeling. She said that she was con-cerned that her brother might be stuck in limbo and roaming the forest for eternity because she heard this happens with those who die accidentally or before their time. I asked her if she wanted me to show her how she could help bring him to the Light, if she really felt that he was stuck. She agreed, and I guided her in a meditation. As we were meditating, she abruptly opened her eyes and told me she had received an explanation of why her brother had communicated with her family when they visited his memorial site in the woods. She said that she was the last person to say good-bye, and that is why he returned. She said he was never stuck, just watching over the area, waiting for the time she decided to visit, as her sister had; so everything was fine. Phyllis thanked me for listening and said she now believes in Spirits but she is still not sure about reincarnation. When she left my booth, her body appeared much lighter.

Phyllis allowed herself to receive the answer to her question, whether her brother was stuck or not after she listened to the answers sent by Sweet Spirit.

"Praying is talking to God. Meditating is listening to God."

This story definitely covered my body with a super case of chill bumps, even though it was an unusual hot 80 degrees.

"Whatever you ask in prayer believe that you have received and it shall be yours." Mark 11:24

* * * * *

On the return trip from a working tour of the West Coast, I found myself sitting across from a woman I just knew had something special to tell me that would become a passage in my book. I spoke with her for a while and she told me her name was Linda and she was a Youth coordinator at the Diocese of Brownsville, in Alamo, Texas. She bestowed upon me her inspiring story.

Linda was scheduled to be at the Oklahoma Federal Building on the day of the infamous bombing, but for *some reason* she delayed her trip by one day. The next day, she went on ahead to Oklahoma and stood in front of what was left of a building that once contained, not only living breathing men and women, but children as well. She felt the urge to look to the sky, and pictured in her heart's eye, (knowing with your heart not the analytical part of the brain), clouds in the distance surrounded by Angels and

Spirits, as they watched the events taking place down below. Each soul was given the chance to know their physical body had been found before going home. It also allowed them to see the closure it brought to their loved ones. She felt this closure was an important factor before they would let the Angels take them home! She watched as Angels took the hands of each soul, and lifted their Angelic energy into heaven with such grace and glory that it brought tears to her eyes.

Listening to her intuition helped keep this woman safe from an untimely death and allowed her to share in the history of sadness that will be encapsulated in our minds throughout time.

After her inspiring story I explained how the experience of seeing Angels sitting on clouds was similar to my own vision which led to the design of the first book cover. She said, "Now I feel chills racing through me."

Moving on with Speed into the Next Millennium

"When I walk down the corridor of life's grand rewards, my life knows no bounds."

The year 2000 is just around the corner and the following information will give you that extra nudge, when you feel the pace toward moving on with your life is going too slowly for you and all concerned.

Whenever I am searching for a new experience or feel it is time to move on to a new project, I advise The Universe that I am open and ready for my next move. I am constantly in awe at how fast my request is answered!

Once, after professing that statement, I opened an issue of "Uptown Express," (now called Uptown Health and Spirit) a local Houston magazine and saw an article about a woman named Sharon Forrest who had come to Houston from Canada to teach a class called "Complete Body Alignment," a procedure that came to her in a dream. After asking guidance for my next move and reading the word 'complete' in C.B.A.; this technique certainly sounded like the perfect answer. The class cost $275, a sum I did not have at the time, but I had finally learned,

"Do it and the money comes, not, I'll do it when the money comes."

I went ahead and signed up for the class. I knew that as long as I had the intention to participate, the money would come quickly, as it had so many times before. Sure enough, on the last day of the class, I sold enough jewelry to the attending students to pay for the cost of the class and more.

The next weekend, I put together my own class and even though it was my first attempt, I received enough guidance and help from my Universal helpers that made the class a success!

Information on C.B.A. can be found in Appendix II.

Learn How To Spell Success

"If you don't know how to spell success,
how can you expect to succeed?"

This phrase came about when I was attempting to type the word success. I asked myself, "Is there one c or two; one e or two?" I heard my inner voice say, "How can you expect to have success if you can't even spell it." Listening to this type of advice is how most of my life and this book has evolved.

I went about putting together other classes, but it seemed that when I called others about taking it, they would reply, "I can't promise I will come because there are so many other classes and speakers to choose from," or "I cannot be in five places at once, and I'm finding it difficult to decide whose class or workshop to attend." With that, I put together a class with a unique format; one where five teachers would come together and share their lessons and messages all in the same place. I decided to have the class at the Ram Das Ashram, a local meditation and Yoga center run by the Sikhs of Houston. Usually the Sikhs do not rent space to non-members but thanks to Hadi Kirn Khalsa whom I call "Angel," I was given permission to have the class there.

I taught for two hours, followed by a pot luck lunch. The other teachers lectured on their particular expertise for the remainder of the day. These classes were held the second Saturday of each month, for nine months, at a donation of $25. I chose to have only nine sessions because in numerology, the number 9 represents completion. This concept worked well, and I met several gifted teachers whom I might not have had the opportunity to know if I had been teaching by myself. I also feel this method of teaching helps those students who are indecisive or find it a more cost effective way to participate in a class. I am happy to hear Louise Hay also used this concept as I found out later.

On the Road again:

After my first C.B.A. class, I was given the message to "Go on the road." I was also told, "Build it and they will come." This uplifting message helped me to understand that all I had to do was appear and a class would easily be formed. I wonder if my Guides also saw the movie 'Field of Dreams,' where that phrase came from, or if writer W. P. Kinsella received this message from his Guides, during the writing of his book, *Shoeless Joe?*

My new car really came in handy, too. I felt comfortable and at peace knowing there would be no driving mishaps during what I surmised would be a massive undertaking. Luckily, I was able to map out most of my itinerary before the trip. I learned of a pen pal organization that connects those wanting to visit other states and countries with locals. From their booklet, I located the places in which I felt guided to teach along the way to my final destination, California. I focused on starting in Dallas, although I was not sure why until I received a flyer advertising Louise Hay's seminar featuring Dr. and Mrs. Jompalski, Shakti Gawain, Wayne Dyer and others. This was the reason I was being led to start my tour there.

I really enjoyed listening to all these gifted speakers but throughout the seminar, I had the feeling that someone was staring at me from behind. I turned around and a woman flashed me a big smile. During the lunch break, she walked over to me and asked if she could join me. At the time, I was sitting on a small bench eating lunch by myself, which is rare because I usually prefer to share my space with others. I was curious why she asked to join me (there is always a reason, and I am always open to find out what they are) so, I invited her to sit down. She said, "I don't know who you are or what you do, but I feel connected to your energy and I feel there is something I have to learn from you." I told her I was facilitating a Complete Body Alignment class and she was welcome to join.

I went back to the conference and by the time it was over I met five other willing candidates to add to my Dallas C.B.A. class. Most of them were teachers in their own right, ready and willing for that next push to help move them past whatever was keeping them stuck. I enjoy teaching the teachers who continue the great work of getting themselves and their students back on the path.

This was the start of a very synchronized trip!

After Dallas, I ventured on to Amarillo. Through the pen pal magazine I met Janet who invited me to stay with her. When I arrived, she gave me the name of her massage therapist, who I called and explained the advantages of her clients and students taking the C.B.A. class. She said it definitely sounded interesting enough for her to suggest to her Yoga class. She even offered the space where she held her classes. Within hours, she called some of her clients, and the next day we had a remarkable class.

Before leaving for my next destination, I gave myself a free day and Janet took me to Lubbock for the evening. On the way, she confided that she had not allowed herself to make any new friends since ending a two-year relationship a year ago. Because of her existing pain, she was happy to be with her dog who even accompanied her to work. She thanked me for helping her to open her heart and to once again feel the desire to socialize past working hours. I told her that I received a message that she would be happy to hear, "Shortly you will travel to Dallas where you will meet someone who will guide you through the transition of releasing the past, leading to emotional and physical freedom." She said that this confirmed a trip she had only thought of taking to Dallas during the up-coming Memorial Day weekend. I called her after that weekend to find out if she had gone on the predestined trip to Dallas. She said, "The guided message was 'right on.' I went to a bar in Dallas and cupid's arrow found its mark." She added, "We are taking turns visiting each other on weekends." Six months later they were living together in Amarillo.

Nothing stops the 'miracle wheels' in motion when two souls are meant to meet. If she had decided to remain closed to the message, she would have had to wait, God knows how long, for another window of opportunity to meet this special person. But because she went with her feelings, our brief connection was a triumph for both of us; she gave me a place to stay and helped me by introducing me to her masseuse, and in return I helped her to see that it is OK to open a heart that had been long closed by one she had loved and lost.

"When you open your heart, you soar like an eagle."

My next stop was Santa Fe, New Mexico. Before starting my trip, I had negotiated with Libby, the owner of an enchanting Bed & Breakfast, to stay for a few days in exchange for attending my C.B.A. class. I especially enjoyed visiting a room that was completely built in quartz crystal. The room contained copper pyramids that are stimulating to sit under during meditation.

The following day, Libby introduced me to Sandra a teacher who held various classes in her home. Sandra introduced me to her students and I talked to them about the benefits of C.B.A. Sandra encouraged them to take the class and most did. The class was scheduled two days later.

The day of the class, Sandra told me that after I walked into her home and our eyes met, she felt that what she was to learn from me would cause a dramatic change in her life. Her insight turned out to be correct. During her time in Theta, Sandra received an awareness that prompted her to run over to me and give me a big hug. When the class was over she told me that for months she had been doing a great deal of work on releasing and was surprised that there was such an intense darkness still existing within her body. I shared with her that during her C.B.A., I was informed that the dark force she met was a past life energy from a time filled with discontent. Sandra said she now realized that this unwanted energy was what was keeping her from becoming the teacher she knew she was brought here to be. She was so happy that she was now ready and completely able to help herself and the students who seek her out for guidance.

"If you keep yourself in the shadows you will remain in the dark."

Being a part of her transformation was a wonderful experience too. When I facilitate a group I advance along with everyone else.

* * * * *

My next C.B.A. in Santa Fe was with a German Shiatsu Master, Ingrid. Since she could not find a partner in order to participate in the main class, I worked with her individually. Generally I prefer to facilitate in couples so I am free to watch for the unusual, but occasionally I am guided to work with a single person. One-on-one sessions have gone way beyond my expectations especially when a person needs complete undivided attention from the Guides as Ingrid did.

When Ingrid went into Theta, I watched as her fingers and legs curled up. I was told that her body had physically re-con-nected with a past life from a childhood disease during a life in India, where her hands and legs were both crippled. Before our session, she had said that she felt there was an energy blockage that disturbed her during her work with her clients. When she returned to a conscious state, we went over the past life where she had a crippling childhood disease in India that she was now aware of.

Ingrid shared a long hug with me and told me she knew that we had to work together in order for the memory of this life and her transformation to take place. She said she was elated and grate-ful to me in helping her to let go of that debilitating, intrusive force. To thank me for her remarkable experience, she took me to Taos for lunch. This was a town I had not planned on visiting but enjoyed it immensely; especially when we stopped to hug a few pine trees. If you can find pine trees that are at least 25-ft. from the road, (the pollution factor) go hug one. The powerful energy shar-ing is worth the effort.

The next day, Ingrid took me to a flea market a few miles out-side of Santa Fe. I walked around, not seeing anything I had not seen before at other flea markets, when I came across a man selling my most favorite thing to buy; gemstone jewelry. He was selling racks and racks of mounted stones. I felt like a kid in a 'rock candy store.' I did not have much money but I did have my mother's beautiful gold, emerald, and diamond ring, which I had not been able to sell. Whenever I showed the ring to jewelers and gold buyers they said they would only buy the piece if they could separate the diamond and emeralds from its settings, thus destroying my mother's favorite ring. I knew she would not have wanted 'her design' ruined, therefore, I understood she would only release the ring to the person who would appreciate it for its beauty. I asked the jeweler if he would be willing to trade Mom's ring for some of his work. He quickly said, "Yes, I would be happy to trade. I've been wondering what I would give my wife on Mother's Day!" I had completely lost track of what a special Sunday this was. The perfect day for Mom to let go of her ring! I looked up and silently thanked Mom, then handed the ring over to the happy man in trade for many beautiful pieces.

The next day, I went sightseeing through the marketplace in downtown Santa Fe. I felt guided to walk into a gallery I *normally* would never have gone into. In this shop I recognized a woman, Harriet, whom I remembered when she taught in Houston. I explained to her that I was staying at a Bed & Breakfast but my designated time there was over. She suggested I stay at her spacious villa for the remainder of my stay. Harriet's home just happened to be located across the street from Sandra's home! It seems The Universe was keeping me in close proximity to where my Guides knew I needed to be! Harriet told me she worked part-time at the gallery between her healing classes at her house. If I had not gone into the shop, I would have missed an opportunity to teach in her home.

The day I was to leave Santa Fe, Harriet invited me to participate in one of her ongoing classes. I had thought my next stop was going to be Albuquerque, but sometimes The Universe keeps me longer than expected in a certain place. I waited with anticipation to see what The Universe had in store for me next!

During Harriet's class we sat in a circle and shared what was going on in our lives. Maya, shared that she needed our help; her bladder had fallen and she was going into the hospital the next day for surgery.

Now I understood why I was kept in Santa Fe for those two extra days before heading on to Sedona!

When the class ended, I located a partner to help Maya and we set a room up for a C.B.A. session. When Maya went into Theta, I saw a tumor the size of a walnut where the doctors were going to operate. When I facilitate, I see images on a screen as if I am watching television. I felt that when her doctors made an incision, the tumor would have spread. Suddenly, a clear blue sky turned dark with thunder and lightening and I watched as Maya, along with the help of the storm's energy, literally released the tumor. Once that was completed, the sun returned bright as ever.

I remembered it stormed during the entire weekend I was learning C.B.A. *When the sky opens and performs its magical light show, wondrous releases are amplified tenfold.* My vision was confirmed when Maya told me she had seen a tumor the size of a walnut and released it.

This electrifying incident, witnessed by the three of us, was definitely a powerful experience.

After the C.B.A., Maya shared with us that she was angry with her husband. I explained to her that the bladder represents being 'pissed off' and her miracle happened because she was *ready* to release, an important factor towards healing and releasing stored anger relating to any dis-ease within the body. It is also wise to make sure the body, mind and spirit are working in peak form and harmony, before exposing the body to the invasive physical insult of surgery. In addition, the recovery time is speedier.

The next stop was Sedona, Arizona

I stayed with Pat, a letter carrier. Pat was not into metaphysics but I was happy to have a place to stay, as I waited for the message about who was to help me put together my next Complete Body Alignment class and where.

After settling in at Pat's house, I went on a tour of Sedona's three metaphysical book and crystal stores. I went into the first store and glanced around at all the beautiful stones while 'waiting for a sign.' Finally, I overheard a woman use the word "psychic" to the cashier. I knew this had to be my sign! I walked over to her, introduced myself and explained that I was in Sedona to teach a class called Complete Body Alignment. She was so interested in what I had to say, that she offered to open her spacious house, call up some of her friends and tell them about the class.

After I got her phone number and directions to her house, I noticed that a psychic fair was going on in the backyard of the store. I wandered out back because I felt there was someone else I needed to meet before I left. I walked over to a woman, and I introduced myself. She introduced herself as Sylvia. I said that I had written to a lady named Sylvia who had sent me information on everything I wanted to know while visiting Sedona. She beamed, "That was me!" I gave her a big hug and told her that I was putting together a Complete Body Alignment class. She told me she went to Sharon Forrest's class when she taught in Sedona last year, but did not remember the important hand positions. I told her that if she helped me facilitate my upcoming class, there would be no charge for her. She agreed, and thanks to my two new friends, the class was quickly formed. Friends told friends and soon I had 12 students, including a mother with her 12 year old girl (the youngest I had worked with so far). Altogether I completed two classes; the other class was formed by a message therapist I met in a health store.

Before I left for California I treated myself to a movie. At that time, there was only one theater in Sedona. At night, the movie theater became a weekly meeting place for the townspeople. I discovered this as I sat in a chair near the auditorium entrance way, and watched as the people entering hugged each other. I am glad I arrived early to watch a scene that was more entertaining than the movie itself; I also recognized a few who had taken my C.B.A. class. I was happy to get a second chance to say good-bye to my new friends.

* * * * *

So on to Los Altos, California, the midpoint of my tour.

I completely understand that The Universe has everything planned out before I arrive at my designated locations.

Here again, through the pen pal magazine, I met still another woman. However, this encounter did not work out at all; we were simply not compatible. Consequently, I chose to leave on the Memorial Day weekend even though I knew driving on a holiday would be a mistake. But moving on was definitely better than staying and being miserable. I also felt this was a lesson on knowing when it was time to leave a bad situation before it got intolerable. In the past, I might have stayed just to be nice, suffering the whole time — *not anymore!*

"Face your obstacles with full empowerment."

From Los Altos, I decided to travel the scenic, Highway 1. I was right on the mark about the holiday traffic because it came to a standstill near Santa Barbara. Glancing about I saw a Best Western motel on my right. I pulled in and the woman at the check-in desk noticed my 'harmony-balancing bracelet.' These bracelets, I am guided to create, brings about a sense of well being to the wearer. They contain as many as fifteen different stones, and an animal fetish. I asked her if she was interested in buying one and she was. Her purchase helped pay for the room that night. Although I had given up a free room with strings in Los Altos, I still ended up with a place to stay. The Universe supported my decision and as usual I was taken care of.

Other than my journey home by way of Tucson, I had not been given a message to go anywhere in particular, when I started for home Memorial weekend day.

As I was driving, I noticed signs for Palm Springs. I thought, "That's the city with all those famous people." And thought nothing more of it until I sensed the message, *"You must teach in Palm Springs"* when I reached the last Palm Springs exit. Never before had I heard my Guides use the words, "you must" in a sentence — it is usually a suggestive feeling. I kept driving and since I did not heed their strong message, they took matters into their own 'spiritual hands.' I felt the steering wheel being turned to the right and I was being led off the highway.

I soon found myself being spirited down the road to my next encounter; of what kind I did not have a clue!

Before reaching whatever my destination was, I stopped at the travelers' information center thinking, "I need a map to get around." But what I really needed was a 'sign,' to help me under stand why I was being brought to Palm Springs!

When I walked into the bureau office, I saw a six foot poster of Sonny Bono, who was the mayor of Palm Springs at the time. I collected all the maps and information *I thought* I needed and drove on into town.

Occasionally, I forget that my spiritual guidance system is much better than any map, compass or travel agent. When I just get out of their way, I am guided to where I need to go at that moment in time.

Suddenly I remembered The Universe's message that helped me in the past, "Those with crystals will be your guide." So when I drove into town and saw a quartz crystal store, I stopped and spoke to the owner. I explained to her about C.B.A. and she said it sounded interesting, but she and her husband were too busy running the store, and doubted if they could be of any assistance to me at all. Before leaving the store, I asked if there was a vegetarian restaurant nearby, and she told me about a health food store just up the road that served tasty food.

It turned out she was more help than she could have imagined.

When I walked into the health food store, I got the notion to head toward the back where I located the restaurant. I noticed two women standing behind the food counter. I looked into the eyes of one of the women and said, "Hi! My name is Tara. I'm traveling across country from Texas putting together classes, when I was literally pulled off the road and delivered to this health store and I have no earthly idea why!"

She stared at me in amazement and said, "Well, what took you so long? I've been praying for you!" That was a sign I could grasp, and thanks to her kindness, I had a place to stay while putting together my classes.

Her name was Nancy and she was a massage therapist who was productive in her profession until fear had taken over her life. She became terribly worried after her 18 year old son who had came back home after a drinking and drug binge. I suggested that she and her son take the Complete Body Alignment class. I explained to her, "You and your son can work out any issues in Theta and when you complete the session, what is left is pure love for you and your partner."

It is so wonderful to watch those who are not even talking to each other before class, skyrocket across a room into each other's arms when they feel 'the essence of love' drawing them together. This is exactly what happened between Nancy and her son in her apartment that day.

That was my first class in Palm Springs and just the beginning.

I taught in Palm Desert, Desert Hot Springs and several other surrounding small towns including Joshua Tree. The lady who runs a famous teaching facility in Joshua Tree heard about my C.B.A. classes and invited me to stay with her. While I was visiting, a teaching slot opened up. Sounds just like what happened to me when I called the Capricorn Center in Kauai! People come from all over to teach at her facility that was constructed completely without any metal. I considered it an honor to be able to work there. After I returned to Palm Springs, Nancy from the health store introduced me to Ralph, a hypnotherapist who conducted a weekly meditation group she frequented on Thursdays. I went to one of his group meetings and met a man who worked with AIDS patients. In the past, whenever I attempted to help those with AIDS, I was thwarted. When I asked Sweet Spirit what that was all about, the message I received was, "You are to work with the living." Back in 1993 AIDS was still in the quick killing stage as opposed to now. When I met this helper of the AIDS community, I took this as a sign to work with them. We made arrangements that evening to hold a C.B.A. class the following Saturday at his home. I called him on Friday to confirm the class, but all I got was a busy signal. Eventually I gave it up to The Universe for the good of all concerned.

When I arrived on Saturday, as previously planned, he looked surprised to see me. I asked him if his students had arrived. He said, "When I hadn't heard from you, I thought you weren't coming, so I canceled the class." I told him I made several attempts to call him only to receive a continuous busy signal. He had no response, so I left.

I took this as a wake-up call, and the completion of an unscheduled three-week-stop-over. From his house I went directly to the motel that I stayed at to relax on my last weekend in Palm Springs; packed up the car and headed to where I knew would be the last stop of the tour, Tucson.

* * * * *

I had driven thousands of miles within this two-month tour, from Houston to California and back. By the time I reached Tucson, my back was in need of some T.L.C. I did not have anyone in particular to stay with so I stayed the night and checked out the next morning

But as usual, I knew something would turn up!

After checking out, I drove around the town for about 15 minutes waiting for a sign when I happened across a health food store. While walking around the store, I noticed a woman drinking orange juice so I walked up to her and nonchalantly said, "Oh, drinking and walking, that's a fun thing to do." I do not know why I said those dumb words; they just came rolling out! When I was in the check out line to pay for my groceries, I noticed the same woman I had just spoken to standing in front of me, so I took this as the sign. I asked her if she knew a massage therapist. She said she did but not one who worked on Sunday. I told her I had just checked out of my hotel and was in need of a massage, or I would not be able to continue my long drive back to Texas. She said, "Why don't you stay at my place, and I'll find someone to massage you on Monday?" Another great connection, as usual!

After the massage, I drove back to the health store as I had a feeling there was someone else I needed to meet before leaving for home. While I was eating lunch, a woman walked up to me and asked if she could sit down and share something with me. She told me she was a Rabbi and one of her duties was to visit prisons; giving solace to the inmates. She asked what brought me to Tucson, and I told her I had driven in from California and was on my way back to Texas after a long teaching tour. She asked if I would do her a favor. When I told her yes, she handed me a dollar bill and said, "As soon as you pass into Texas, put this dollar into the hand of the first street beggar you see holding out a hand to you." I thought this was a strange request, but by now, knowing how the Angels I meet on my travels think, it was really not that unusual. When I reached El Paso, I stopped for lunch. I was just about to return to the highway, when I noticed a man standing on the sidewalk *holding out his hand*! I knew this was the one the Rabbi had in mind for her simple gift, definitely with angelic strings. I held out the bill, placed it in his hand and informed him, "This dollar come's all the way from Tucson, Arizona, to you, personally, from a special lady." Our eyes locked as he silently looked at me completely dumbfounded. As I drove on, I stared into the rear view mirror, watching him as he continued to stare at my car until he was a blur.

I truly believe this man's whole lifestyle, including his probable feelings of "Why is life passing me by" was changed by this 'chill bump' intervention — the day he chose to receive this miracle from Sweet Spirit.

This inspiring incident helped us both that day to understand the words, "GOD LOVES YOU BABY!" as Della Reese so eloquently says on the TV show, "Touched by an Angel."

This was the way my inspirational sojourn unfolded. A community of souls, with open hearts and minds, shared themselves with me and others so we could hear "The words of The Universe,"

"With complete trust, all things go smoothly."

This trip truly taught me that when we open to our inner guidance, The Universe backs you 100%, especially when your intentions are filled with Love and Light, as this "adventure in faith" showed me.

"Intention is a map for the mind."

I thrive on living in the now, unaware of what my next mission will be, but open to whatever my Guides want and wherever the assignments take me. This is just a taste of what living in the now can do for you too!

CHAPTER 10

Bringing in the Angel Babies

All God's children who have chosen a life of service.

Childbirth is a blessed experience for every woman who chooses it. Any midwife will tell you giving birth is a natural function of a woman's body. As with many other physical functions, emotional issues sometimes hamper this miracle. Many women have come to me after seeking out a multitude of ways offered to them on becoming pregnant without success. I do, however, believe in miracles and perfect timing. Although the women who have come into my space asking me for guidance have become pregnant, I do not claim to cause this to happen. What I do do is help them and their partners 'tune in' so they will *truly* understand the reasons stopping them from their goal — bringing in their own "Angel Babies." I also assist mothers-to-be when the child is late or in trouble.

There are several reasons why a woman may be unable to conceive, even after they have gone through great lengths.

- Emotional disturbances between husband and wife may alienate the baby's soul. Constant bickering constitutes an unhealthy environment.
- Only one partner putting in the energy needed toward the goal of bringing in life. Remember, "It takes two, baby!"
- The soul of the child is not ready to come to the chosen parents or, if it comes, it does not stay long. Even these souls have free will and sometimes they change their minds or are scared about returning to Earth *to accomplish their lessons*. This might be one reason for crib deaths, because these enlightened ones come in, quickly understand what their assignments are and leave.

• One or both of the parents fear something on some level. Maybe they fear not knowing how to care for their child or that they may not be good parents. They could fear reverting back to their *still unresolved ways* because of the way their parents treated them. I have helped couples understand and release whatever their fear was. Babies are not brought to us to help keep a marriage together or as a source of company for a lonely person. They are brought here for love, learning and future independence; solely, to be allowed to become all they can be.

During a Massage Therapy Conference, a friend in her eighth month was helping me. She informed me that her doctor had told her that her placenta was too close to her stomach, which might cause her to need a Cesarean if the problem did not correct itself. I communicated to her baby girl that I needed her help in pushing the placenta away from her Mom's stomach. This was my first time performing this highly unusual hands-on procedure, successfully I might add, on a woman only weeks away from her due date.

* * * * *

I remember meeting another mother-to-be whose baby refused to make an appearance and was almost a month overdue. I placed my hand on her stomach to communicate with the baby and find out why he had not arrived. The message that I felt from the baby was, "Grandpa hates me!" I thought, what an unusual statement for an unborn to be thinking, so I asked the woman, "Why does your baby feel his grandfather hates him?" "Well," she said, "Maybe because my father is always talking down to him. Since I'm not married, he keeps calling him a bastard." I said, "The baby doesn't feel good about being called names and refuses to be born into such an angry environment."

I suggested that she go home and tell her father that his grandson refuses to be born into a hostile environment where he is already feeling unloved. She called me a few weeks later and told me that when she explained to her father what his grandson was feeling, he sat down in front of her, placed a hand on her stomach and softly said, "I love you, my boy. You are welcome and wanted. I'm

so sorry I hurt you with my uncaring words, my beloved grandson." After those endearing words, he became a proud grandfather the next day.

Watch what you say around the Unborn, they hear and feel
everything!

* * * * *

When another woman contacted me because her baby girl
was late, I connected with her baby and the message I felt was, "I
don't want to be a Capricorn; I want to be an Aquarian." (She
wanted to be a teacher and a humanitarian for the planet; qualities
Aquarians' are known for) Mom now understood her baby would
make an appearance as soon as Capricorn turned into Aquarius.
Several years later, when I was working at a psychic fair, a darling
long-haired blond child ran into my arms as if she knew me. While
I was hugging her, I looked up and recognized the woman coming towards me as the mother-to-be and the child I was hugging
was her little Aquarian I helped. Mom gave me a big hug and
introduced me to her daughter. The woman said she wished I had
helped her with her second child, because she was also late.

Working with these mothers and their Angel Babies helped me
to understand that unborn babies remember your energy after communicating with them in the womb.

* * * * *

When I traveled to Phoenix in 1997 to take part in a Woman's
Expo, a lady stopped by my table and asked, "Can you help me
become pregnant?" Now, I do not have a sign in my booth stat-
ing, "I help women have babies," or any other sign that says I help
in anyway, but somehow this lady believed I could. *Sometimes that
is all it takes.* I quickly answered, "Yes, I can help you but only if
you are ready and willing to be receptive in bringing in your Angel
Baby." She looked at me as though I were crazy. I waved her in
and said, "Let's find out what is stopping you from what you want."
She stood frozen in front of my booth. I had to come out from
behind my table, take her by the hand and escort her into my
booth. I touched her stomach and the message I shared with her
was, "You will become pregnant in five months, and your "Angel

Baby" has chosen to be born in San Francisco." The woman was elated and said, "Wow, San Francisco! I love San Francisco! What a perfect place for my baby be to born!" This happy woman left with that inspirational message. I truly believe because of this angelic intervention; all came to be.

* * * * *

I was facilitating a Complete Body Alignment class in Houston. When it was finished, I talked with a woman about information I received concerning her only son, now 18, and the heavy burden of guilt she suffered from having four abortions before finally giving birth to him. She shared with me that because of all the guilt she lived with, she felt she never really allowed herself to give her son the love he deserved. The message I was given to help her was, "Your son is the same soul that came to you on those four attempts. He wanted to be with you so much, that he waited until *you* were ready. So feel free to love him and release the guilt that binds you to the past." When she heard those blessed words, it opened up a floodgate of cleansing tears. I held and rocked her until she was done. The next time I saw her, she told me that her relationship with her son was wonderful; she hugs him and tells him that she loves him every chance she gets. By releasing all her guilt, she felt the freedom to start a teaching facility in her home for other suffering mothers and anyone else who needs help.

"Unresolved issues remain as painful experiences."

* * * * *

Once a woman came over and shared with me that when her son was born, the doctor found it necessary to use forceps so the baby's face has been quite disfigured. The evening of his birth, she was holding him and loving him, unconditionally, when the baby's father walked in the room. He asked his wife how she could hold that ugly thing. From that day on, her son always *felt ugly,* thus creating a detrimental misperception about his appearance and the feelings of, "If my father can't love me as I AM; I must be ugly and unlovable, and nobody but my mother will ever love me." For most of his life, whenever he looked into a mirror, all he saw was his perception of an 'ugly man,' although many have commented that he was handsome enough to be a model. Consequently, this beautiful man spent most of his life believing the words his father had proclaimed in front of him on his birth day. The moment he realized how his father's words had vastly affected his body, mind and spirit, he was able to truly see himself as he was — handsome, and truly worthy of love and affection.

"You don't see because you are not looking."

CHAPTER 11

Dreams and Interpretations

"And what they dare to dream of, dare to do," from "Commemoration Ode to poet J.R. Lowell." I heard these words as a teenager and accepted them as a wonderful expression of my life.

A teacher once told me during a dream workshop that we play out all the characters in our dreams. I also believe that whether your characters resemble your parents, actors or your boss, they represent some issue residing deep within your subconscious, which must be addressed, especially if the dreams are recurrent. For example, if you dream you are a famous person or anyone you know, ask yourself, what is it about that person you like or dislike, and you will understand the reason for dreaming about them. It is important for you to interpret your own dreams since everyone has their own agenda and thoughts which may have nothing to do with you. To find the answers to your private visions, past or future events, go within; your own answers are waiting to help you unravel the mysteries of your subconscious.

Ask yourself, "Am I now ready and willing to release all the negative thoughts, unresolved feelings and energy that may not be for my Highest Good?"

When you are ready, use these dream therapy methods:

1. After closing your eyes say, "I will remember my dreams upon awakening." Even though some feel they do not dream at all, we dream three times. Once after slipping into sleep mode from Alpha state, once while in R.E.M. or Theta state, and once as you are coming back into a waking state, Beta.

2. Keep a small hand held tape recorder close to your bed to record your comments and memories. You only have about 30 seconds in which you remain in a sleepy state (almost fully awake, Beta state). By the time you turn on the light and reach for a pen and paper you probably have forgotten it all. Record as much of the dream as possible. Do not worry about accuracy or grammar; you just want to record as much as you can of the main story of each dream. When you finish recording your dream, ask yourself "What is this dream telling me?" and record that.

3. You may consider using a dream book to look up certain symbols, but authors, compiling their information, do not know *you*, so remember, it is all open to their interpretation. Go within to find your own truths. If you wish to use a book, I recommend *The Dreamer's Dictionary* containing over 3,000 symbols, by Lady Stearn Robinson & Tom Corbett.

4. After you have recorded everything you remember, go over the tape and pick out all the significant symbols; the characters, colors and any unusual movements and emotional feelings, i.e., love, happiness, fear, anger, hate; anything that will help alert you to any hidden messages. Now record or write all this down. By now you are fully in Beta, wide awake stage, so go over everything and start your evaluations.

Dreams and their interpretations:

In one of my dreams, there was something wrong with one of my car's tires. When I woke up, I checked all the tires to make sure everything was all right. I did not see anything wrong with them, but to be safe in case it was a precognitive dream, foretelling important events or danger, I went to my mechanic and had them checked out. After all four tires were examined, the mechanic informed me that he had found a small nail in the right front tire. While the tires were off, they also checked the brakes and found only 10% of the brake pad left, which was not safe. This dream helped me prevent two problems from becoming more serious if left unchecked.

I delved into what my dream wanted to tell me, on an emotional level. This is how I broke it down: The car is my emotional body. The problematic tire was on the right side, the male side: moving ahead, as opposed to your left side, the female side: receiving and nurturing. Without proper movement (the tires) I cannot move forward with ease. Without good brakes I was unable to stop or put a stop to whatever I was involved in, which may not be for my Highest Good.

I interpreted it as, "I was not moving ahead *with any great speed*." So I asked, "What is stopping me from moving on?" Guidance reminded me that I was in a "going-nowhere-relationship." Since I had refused to put a *stop* to it, it has kept me from moving on or bringing anyone else in for something better. So give yourself a *break;* it will improve your chances of happiness.

In another dream, I was holding a bottle of potassium pills in one hand and a banana, also full of potassium, in the other. Since that dream, I have been eating bananas and taking B-6 almost every day. Diabetes runs on Mom's side of the family, and I read that those with diabetes have a deficiency of B-6 and potassium. Through this dream I was probably releasing my fear of contracting diabetes, which I refuse to bring into my life by taking care of myself.

Recurrent dreams mean that we have refused to listen or tune into the issues, our dreams are making an effort to bring to our attention. Our subconscious mind will keep repeating this information until we open and receive the message. Our Higher Self knows that we are not consciously aware of this troublesome denial. These powerful expressions of communication definitely help us by getting our full attention through repetition, until we are willing to understand there is a problem that must be addressed.

In one of my recurrent dreams, I was in my car driving to a destination. I parked and walked to where I was being led. When I was ready to return to my car, no matter how hard I concentrated, I was unable to remember where I parked it. I felt stressed and confused. I have had this dream at least twice a year for as long as I can remember. When I wake up, I ask, "So what does not finding the way back to my car really mean?" My perception of this dream is, I arrive to my destinations in life just fine but I am unable to find my way back. The answer was to keep moving ahead. "It's not important where you have been, it's more important where you are going. Stay on your path."

> *"Heal the past, live in the now and the future
> is yours to command."*

Whenever I forget their message, the dream will always come back to remind me to "Stay on the path!" Sometimes it is an Angelic reminder to "Lighten Up!"

* * * * *

I was driving down a highway in Florida. I stop because I cannot decide to go left on Highway 9 or to go right on Highway 1. I finally decided to go left. Up the road I started to feel that I was going in the wrong direction. I stop at a convenience store and ask the proprietor, "Am I going the right way?" He says, "No, you need to turn around and go back to Highway 1 — that's the path for you now."

In Numerology, 1 means beginnings and 9 means completion. So, when I turned left on Highway 9, the receiving, nurturing, female side, I opened to receive a message from myself. "You must complete before you can begin."

What this dream was telling me was before I can begin my journey there must be closure. I left a relationship unresolved when I left Florida.

Remember, in a dream, all the characters are *you* as they appear as part of a life stage in which you are playing out the many parts and facets that you must push through from your allusive subconscious realm in order for you to see and understand.

* * * * *

I had many dreams about Shirley MacLaine in 1996

In one dream, we were walking on a beach, talking. In another dream, I was visiting with her, along with others, during a gathering at her home in Malibu. When the group was leaving she took my arm and said, "No, we have not finished yet." In the third dream, Shirley and I passed each other in the hallway of a large office building; I was going up the stairs and she was coming down, headed toward a large windowed door. When I recognized her, I turned and screamed out, "Shirley, it's me!" She answered, "No, you must be mistaken." The next day, I explained this dream to Marva, a psychic friend working for Shirley in California. Marva said that Shirley had been keeping a low profile in the metaphysical circles. This dream certainly proved what Marva said was true. I had not received flyers for any of her upcoming workshops or events as I had in the past. Shortly after that dream, Shirley started appearing more often on stage and in films.

After those dreams there were other occurrences involving Shirley which lead me to think that I was meant to work with her.

I was sitting for my portrait at the Glassell School of Art in Houston, when the artist took a break, I peeked at the canvas. I was surprised to see Shirley's face staring back at me. Upon the artist's return, I asked her why she would paint Shirley MacLaine while looking at me; she had no explanation. During the next sitting, within five strokes, the artist quickly changed Shirley's picture into one that bore my resemblance!

Another incident involving Shirley occurred one day when I was drawn to a vegetarian restaurant which I frequented often. I walked into the restaurant and made eye contact with a woman I knew had something important to share with me. I sat back to back to her at the next table. While I waited for my food, I turned around, tapped her on the shoulder and said, "I feel you are tired, but there is still an exciting energy about you. What's going on?" She said, "Yesterday I was with a group that included Shirley MacLaine." I said, "That's interesting because I've been dreaming about her quite often, and I was feeling that these dreams may be telling me that I should work with her." She asked, "Why don't you call or write to her? Shirley once told me about another woman who felt the same way. She wrote her and now works with her." She asked if I wanted Shirley's address and telephone number. With a surprised grin I answered yes and thanked her for being a great messenger.

I chose to write Shirley instead of calling her. A response came back almost too quickly as if it were sent on the wings of Angels. Upon beautiful baby blue stationery was typed,

"These are such exciting times we live in and my most important lesson has been to understand that a positive and productive life is up to each one of us *individually*. We are our own realizers; we are own best teachers.

Remember to keep the knowingness that the God source is within you. Trust it and your life and love will reflect it!"

She ended the letter with Love and Light as I always do.

After receiving her letter, I felt inspired to venture out on my own, to be "My own teacher and best realizer."

CHAPTER 12

Seeing Into The Future

Messages come into my mind's eye whenever I ask The Universe a question or when I am open and receptive to the voices in my head.

This prophecy came to me in 1995 after wondering if a woman will ever be elected President of the United States. I have learned that when you ask a question in an explicit manner, you will always receive the correct answer. My inner voice said, "The first female president will be the reincarnation of Eleanor Roosevelt." I thought that was fantastic, with all her accomplishments as our Ambassador and Stateswoman, including the other services she executed, in presidential style, as president Roosevelt's right hand woman.

I shared the story about Mrs. Roosevelt with a few friends and associates. One day, the moment I mentioned Eleanor Roosevelt's name to a friend on the phone, I felt heavy duty Universal chill bumps. I received another message that said, "Eleanor Roosevelt has just been re-born, and she will be our president in 32 years." I plan to be around to vote for her!

* * * * *

The next prophecy arrived in 1997 concerning Princess Diana.

I came home from a conference unaware of Princess Diana's passing, and walked into the bathroom. On a small piece of paper was written one word, "Diana." I did not think anything of it until I turned on the television and watched as the newscaster talked about the car wreck. Whenever I get two consecutive alerts such as this, I know "something is afoot" (As Sherlock Holmes would say to Watson.) I asked, "What are y'all wanting me to know about

Diana?" (My guides love when I talk Texan!) I received the message, *"Diana is the Princess who will be Queen."* I said, "How about an interpretation to this puzzle?" (They love word and mind games.) The answer was, "William's firstborn will be a female, and this female will once again be our Diana." This meant, when Diana returns she will be a true Princess. This will make her '*the Princess who will be Queen,*' and Britain will prosper." This message had the energy patterns of Merlin as he worked closely with 'The Royals of Ye Old Britain.' I was also told, "She came to teach Prince William to be a great king and his daughter, in the future, could be the Queen of England." Later I received the message that Prince William would marry at the age of 25. It all sounds feasible to me, and I receive the 'chill bumps of yore' every time I share this story.

When Marianne Williamson came to speak on her latest book at Unity Church in Houston, she mentioned Diana's name during the first half of her lecture. As soon as I heard Diana's name, I took that as a sign and wrote on a small piece of pink paper the message I had received about her a few days earlier to pass on to Marianne. When Marianne took a break, I walked up to the stage and told her I had a message about Diana that I wanted to share with her. She reached out her hand to take the slip of paper. As we both held on to it, I felt electricity running through my body and my hair stood up higher than usual. (On some level, I know how "The Highlander" feels after he absorbs another immortal's energy force!) It was also a confirming experience about the coming Queen of England — long live Her Majesty — Queen Diana!

CHAPTER 13

The Wisdom of Crystals & Gemstones

Crystals are not a fad.
Crystal and gemstone healing takes place when we allow our Aura to mix with a particular color stone. Through this dominant energy, our Aura becomes clearer and brighter in color thus removing blocks and helping to reestablish balance and health.

Mankind has used crystals all over the world since before recorded time to heal themselves and their animals. When we harmonize with The Universal energy patterns that come from nature in the shape of minerals and crystals, we can use them as tools to assist in the natural process of healing, balancing and inner growth.

Crystals, gems and other minerals are also wonderful tools for transformation. They can be "solid friends" as well as objects of beauty, helping us along the path to our goals. The most popular in the mineral kingdom are the Quartz Crystal (white), Amethyst (purple), Aventurine (green), Rose Quartz (pink) and Carnelian, a Chalcedony (orange).

Clear quartz helps amplify thought and energy. Beams of energy run through lines of telecommunication amplifying thought, energy and light. This is a good explanation of how psychics are able to use crystals to enhance their abilities over the phone. High amplification of energy is the reason why crystals are used in laser beams, computers, watches and more.

Sadly, a powerful quartz laser in the wrong hands was harmful and destructive to Atlantis. Many historians, and those who believed they lived during a past life there, feel that an extremely large and powerful quartz crystal laser beam may have been one cause, if not the main cause, for the island to disappear into the sea.

When dealing with any new form of healing, one needs to approach it with personal thoughts on how to integrate it into one's life. To start your collection, I suggest using the following from God's kingdom:

A clear white Quartz Crystal activates all levels of conscious ness, helps one to see more clearly, dispels negativity and protects when placed on your person, in a pocket, home, computer or on your car's rear view mirror. I recommend keeping a crystal cluster or plate in your home and place of business. Clusters can be used to clear the energy up to 25-ft. and are self-cleaning.

Amethyst quartz balances body, mind and spirit, helps in strengthening the immune system and have a calming and protective quality.

Rose quartz, known as the "Love Stone," provides 'Unconditional Love' of yourself and those around you.

Aventurine quartz enhances one's creativity, reinforces decisiveness, and balances emotions.

Carnelian is used to dispel negativity. Soldiers wore this stone on their breast plates for courage. Also worn by High Priests.

As for caring for your stones, the sun energizes and the moon cleanses. To help clear accumulated negativity, occasionally place them in the freezer for three hours. When you do not have these two methods handy, simply hold the stone in your hand, bring it up to your mouth and say "I call on the 'Breath of God,' and blow on it. This will clean away accumulated negative energy. Continue this method every time you use the stones, especially after a healing session. You can also place stones on a crystal cluster because they are like a city of energy unto themselves and the clusters will clean them.

A good crystal information guide helps you choose the stones and teaches you the parts of the body, mind and spirit they affect. When you carry a crystal with you, you are carrying all elements of creation. God's mineral realm was here before mankind, so allow these old friends to work with you as they were sent to do.

"Just as the rainbow appears in the heaven as a sign of God's love and light to mankind, so does the crystal come forth from the Earth to bring a message of Light from the past as a promise of Love for the future."- Sananda (Jesus Christ)

* * * * *

When I was helping art students unblock their creativity at Rice University's Art History department, my favorite rose quartz disappeared. This stone was from Madagascar, a country filled with specimens, that to me, have stronger stored energy than others I have worked with. I am not quite sure why that is, unless that country has an energy vortex.

It was about six months before I returned to the same department. I went into a storeroom, looking for costumes to use. Before turning on the light, I looked on the floor. In the dark I felt there was something circular on the floor. I bent down and picked up what was drawing my attention. When I turned on the light, to my amazement it was my missing rose quartz; the one I thought I would never see again! Stones definitely have a God-like mind of their own. The stone knew the students needed its healing energy more than I and decided to stay and work *its love magic* on them. When my wonderful 'love stone' greeted me, I was happy that it was ready to return and once again work its love magic with me.

* * * * *

I was in a class with a renowned Crystal Healer from California. She told us how she used Amethyst crystals to remove cancer from the bodies of her clients. During a crystal healing class, she said one of her programmed amethyst stones turned white after absorbing a man's cancer and was dying. She said this was her favorite crystal and prayed that it would come back to her, instead, it exploded. The crystal had absorbed too much for its size to safely handle. She also told us about a time when another healing crystal turned white. This time, she asked the class to encircle the dying amethyst and send it their Love and Light energy. With the help of her students, her stone returned back to its natural purple radiance and continued its destiny of absorbing disease.

You can also program your stones by holding them up to your mouth and telling them how you want them to help you.

* * * * *

Stones will pick you out, when they want to work with a particular person.

I was working a psychic fair in a hotel, when a woman came running up to my table and placed her hand on a stone. "What is this stone?" She asked. "It screamed to me from across the room!" I told her it was called Vanadium and it came from Morocco. She was astonished because she was going there the following week! Even though she could have bought a vanadium stone on her trip for less, she knew she had to buy this one. *She felt it would protect her during her trip.*

* * * * *

One day in my store, a woman came in and picked up a Lapis Lazuli stone in the shape of a heart. She said she did not have the money to buy it that day, but she promised to return the next day if I would hold it. I told her I needed at least a deposit. She said she did not have any money and left disappointed. In the past, people have asked me to hold merchandise and have not returned as promised. When I said no to a new customer I thought I was in my power until I heard the phrase, *"Unless you take a negative and change it into a positive, it will remain a negative."* I was about to remove the heart from the show case and save it for her when another woman walked in and picked up the same heart. I watched as it jumped out of her hand and flew to the floor. She looked at me and asked me how I did that. I picked it up and placed it back into her hand and again it went to the floor. I told her that I had nothing to do with the way it was acting and that it was not meant for her because it belonged to someone else, who, *I now knew*, was returning the next day. She told me she never heard of a salesperson keeping someone from buying before and walked out in a huff. The next day, the first woman, the one the stone really wanted to be with, came back as promised. She was so happy that when she saw the heart still sitting there, she picked it up and kissed it. She told me her boyfriend gave her the money for a birthday gift, and told her to buy something she really wanted. I would say she did just that.

When I am conducting a class and people ask me what stone they should use I tell them to look over all the stones; open to them and they will guide you. They pick you, you do not necessarily pick them. After the students make their choices, I explain why that particular stone wanted to work with them for their Higher Good.

To learn more about crystals I highly recommend the reference book, *Love is In the Earth* by Melody.

* * * * *

As I walked the streets of Greenwich Village on a Sunday morning in May 1989 on my way to Washington Square Park, I noticed six shiny new pennies in the street gutter. I wondered what the chances were of finding so many pennies, lying so uniformly in a line! As I finished that thought, I heard my inner voice say, *"Pick them up; for you will find someone to give them to."*

People flocked to this park to be entertained by the magicians, musicians and acrobats. I entered and walked toward the music. As I neared the musicians, I noticed to my right, a young man in his early 20's, sitting cross-legged on a large gray rock, with a sign behind him that read, *"Poems for Pennies!"* Now I understood the message and the destiny of the planted pennies. I asked the young man his name and if he was willing to compose a poem for these six pennies. He nodded and told me his name was Joe Baral. I poured the pennies into his eager hand and he prepared himself. I watched as his pen quickly flew across the page of his worn notebook.

After a few minutes, I turned back to see how he was progressing. I noticed he had stopped writing and looked perplexed. I felt that his creative fervor had ebbed. I walked over to him and placed my personal Hematite on his left knee and walked back to my seat in silence. I chose that particular stone because of its ability to help unblock creativity, ground and balance one's energies. I was correct in my choice, and within seconds he was back in the flow.

When he finished, he brought not one, but two poems over to me and presented me with his labor of love. He also attempted to hand back my stone. I put up my hand to stop him and told him the Hematite now wanted to work with him. While someone else might have thought me totally bonkers, he smiled with a look of complete understanding. After I read the poems, I asked his permission to publish them. The poet beamed with pride and answered with an excited yes, and thanked me. It has taken me 10 years to publish Joe's poems, but then again 10 in numerology represents new beginnings; for me, and for him.

These are the two poems that Joe Baral, a New York University student from California at that time living in Hoboken, New Jersey, wrote.

The Light within you

Is indeed the Light without?

Why wait for tomorrow

When today is so bright.

Search and search for an answer

When the question is so slight

Life is lived for living

This I know is right.

* * * * *

The wind blows forever

The courtyard has always been

I love to see the sun

Whatever mood I'm in.

CHAPTER 14

It's Good to be an Angel Worker

In the End...

My recognition of coincidences seems to have heightened my senses, and these days I find I am often "guided," to take specific action. Since I was 12, I have felt I was in training; beginning with my dedicated listening to that still small voice that comes to me when I ask for help for myself or others. Recognize that there is a vast knowledge to tap into and develop which will lead to direct actions that help you tune into all that you desire.

The following reflects what I believe is true for us all — we are sent to help heal each other, and can do so when we accept that we are part of the "Celestial Universal Wholeness."

Lessons of coincidences

As you have read, the main theme of this book is to help you to be all you can be, both easily and effortlessly. Since I teach by example, all the stories and in-depth information has been meant to guide you through whatever knowingly or unknowingly has kept you from moving onto the path and life that The Universe meant for you at birth by Divine Right.

We were born perfect in the Creator's eyes but somewhere down the road we became a sponge for unhappy beings and we absorbed their stuff; whether it was for our good or not — definitely for our karmic lessons in this life.

We are not meant to suffer through endless phases of unhappy and unhealthy mental, physical and spiritual abuse. Remember, 'You' are a Child of God, born perfect in every way. Somewhere between birth, childhood and adulthood, you have allowed yourself to muck it up by continuously saying, "I can't," whenever you do not know what to do instead of asking for help from Angels, Guides and Lightworkers. You stop them from helping you because they cannot help unless asked; 'ask and it shall be done.' They are all out there waiting to help.

How to contact all there is in the Universal Realm

The simplest way to contact our Celestial Guides is to *go within and ask*. The Cosmic Realm is not on linear time therefore, it takes only a nano second, to receive that which is for your Highest Good and soul growth, when you openly ask.

Another way to connect with the '*All-Knowing Realm*' is to first, without inhaling expel the stale air, breathe deeply and hold for a count of five, exhale for a count of five, hold for a count of five. Holding your breath this way helps to connect with your Higher Self. Do this five times, as 5 means change. Breathing from the nose (the mouth is for eating and kissing) brings you into Alpha and helps set up a field and path that alerts your helpers that you are preparing to receive them. When you learn how to better use this breathing, extend the breath for a count of 10 bringing you even deeper into a state of knowing bliss or Theta. I use this breathing technique as the pathway before establishing a Touching the Lion On the Nose or C.B.A. link. Next, visualize a personal quiet place, whether a beach or forest where you chose to meet with your Guides for advice. Ask your Guides their names so you may call them at will.

The main characters in my guidance system are *Jesus,* for what ails me at the moment; *Lord Michael,* to separate me from what binds me in an unhealthy situation; *Isis,* for healing after a strenuous teaching tour; *Seth,* healer in alternative methods; *Merlin,* for his magical sense of humor when mine is hiding; *Ganesh,* to remove obstacles; *Lakshmi,* for prosperity and anyone else who wishes to stick in their '*Celestial two pennies worth.*'

There are no special words to say when connecting with your Guides, just tell them what you want and always end with, *this or something better.* They know what is for your Highest Good, even if you do not. They know how to get it to you easy and effortlessly, over and above what is stopping you.

Above all, remember to change all the toxic vocabulary you are tripping over, like the *can'ts* and *don't knows*. Get out of the way, and shout-up to The Universe, "That*'s it! I've had enough!"* all the negativity and problems that surround you when you are feeling stuck, allowing them to transmute into something better. By you surrendering to this powerful feat of love, you feel a grand release beyond imagination. Surrender does not mean giving in, it means *giving it up to a Higher Power to be cleansed.*

Bringing everything out in this book has been a great healing for me. Learning there is a 'Universal Wisdom' has allowed me to grow. With their guidance, I remain safe from those who come into my life to act out and abuse me from past lives or the present one.

"Don't kill the messenger" means it would be for your Highest Good to listen to their impeccable wisdom, helping you to re-connect with God instead of blaming God for 'not listening' as you are the one not listening.

It behooves you to listen to all the teachers that are here to guide you, both on the physical plane and beyond. When you pray, you place your intention out into the Cosmos telling them you are ready and open to their insight. All this gifted information is coming directly from the 'highest Light-source possible' for all concerned. People have said to me, "I want to do what you do." "But ya are, Blanche, ya are!" is my answer—as Betty Davis told Joan Crawford in the movie *Whatever happened to Baby Jane* when Blanche told Jane that she would never treat her in this vile manner if she were not in a wheelchair.

We are all capable of doing what I do. I choose to use this wisdom every waking and sleeping moment — my life works better when I do. Jesus mentioned how powerful "Universal God Energy" is. As He puts it, "What I do, you can do, and greater things than these." This is accomplished when two or more are gathered in His name.

Listed below are the subtle ways The Universe chooses to pass messages on to me, when I am balanced and fine-tuned like a radio, turned on and ready to receive.

- When guided to a particular place and meet someone I need to talk with, or they with me.
- The interpretations I need to unravel mysteries, while in dream state.
- When guiding me to a particular book, magazine or newspaper after asking for help, and reading exactly what I asked for.
- There are also the well-timed actions and encounters when I am guided to someone in need, or a healing after being pulled off the road; approached in health stores or airports; alerted to show up, or call when someone is thinking of me, to a clients amazement.

When a miracle occurs, I feel like an angel in service, and I know that I am giving at the highest level that we all are capable of reaching. No matter what you were brought to Earth to do, this form of service is by far, to me, the greatest and most intuitive of actions.

I find today that I value others more because of my own experiences, and I am more open to healing through change.

"Some have stated that our existence is like the game of life.
I chose to see life as the games or lessons we play out;
since we are all 'God's winning children,' we all win at life."

Open to your Guides and teachers, especially when it feels so warm and fuzzy in your heart of hearts.

"May angels appear at your doorstep!"

After returning from my Kauai trip, tired and sick, Isis reminded me of something I said long ago, after she healed my tired and broken wings,

"Come to us with your broken wings and learn to fly free."

APPENDIX 1
Words of Inspiration

These are quotes from two Astral Travelers:
I AM KUTHUMI

An incarnated master that works with whomever wishes to contact him, in The Universal Realm

I AM a created ray from the very heart of God,

I AM shining each day with the lifting, living Light of resurrection's eternal flame, awakening my divine memory to the infinite WISDOM in a SUNBEAM, a ray-o-light within me, within all men I glory in light's apparent simplicity.

Knowing that therein lies locked the mightiest power,

The most profound wisdom and the greatest love of eternity, my own "I AM presence" ever unlocks for me this wisdom-balanced power, in daily manifestation of all the ascended Jesus Christ love, beauty, grace and perfection now made manifest.

In childlike humility I sit at the feet of the gracious ascended masters until sweetly crowned by them. I AM ever the SUNBEAM RAY that shines for them each DAY!

Peace is within thee, as a little child on the lap of its mother, as a little child so is my soul within me. Peace is with thee.

Words from The Mother Mary:

"Beloved mighty I Am Presence, father of all life, act on my behalf this day. Fill my form. Release the Light that is necessary for me to go forth to do Thy holy will. See that my energies are used to magnify the Lord in everyone whom I meet. See to it that Thy holy wisdom released to me is used constructively for the expansion of God's kingdom. And above all, beloved Heavenly Father, I commend my spirit unto Thee and ask that as Thy Flame is one with my Flame, the union of these two Flames shall pulsate to affect in my world the continuous alertness and attunement, which I feel with my Holy presence, with the Holy Spirit, and with the World Mother."

These mighty words from Mary depict my life's work.

Appendix 2
Complete Body Alignment

A Complete Body Alignment (C.B.A.) is a proven and effective method of directing Universal energy to produce maximum re sults. For centuries, mankind has searched and prayed for avenues to channel their energy in order to obtain healing of the body, mind and spirit for their Highest Good. Millions of dollars are spent annually on hypnotherapy, psychiatric or spiritual Guidance in an endless, and often fruitless, quest for gaining a higher plane of consciousness. C.B.A. is taught in pairs or one-on-one so the participants may learn to receive and direct this God-like energy toward the healing of others. Learning to direct this energy is not a process that takes years to develop nor does it cost a small fortune, all you have to do is be willing to be a receiver for your Highest Good and soul growth.

While in Theta, you will balance the left and right hemispheres of the brain, where our faculties of power and love reside. The energy works with the pituitary and pineal centers and hypothalmus, increasing E.S.P. This balance awakens the energy vortex or "crown," the center of wisdom, enlightenment, understanding, and illumination — the Christ Consciousness.

C.B.A. brings you down into a state of R.E.M., known as the dream state. You are fully aware of your surroundings in this state. Many feel this is deeper than any form of meditation or hypnotherapy that has been used in the past. Ancient wisdom, high master teachers and Guides will be with you. Your Guides assist you by helping you to get in touch with any past lives that keep you from moving on. You may learn secrets from your subconscious that will, on a daily basis, help guide and direct you to make better decisions.

The process takes approximately one hour. In that short span of time, you will feel as if chiropractors, acupuncturists, and Masters of Enlightenment have worked on and with you. There is a healing, cleansing and purifying process that continues to work with you for two weeks after the C.B.A.

All great achievements happen when it is for your Highest Good. I have seen loving pets who have made their transition, appear and help their human friends release at a faster pace. I have also witnessed a form of exorcism when a woman relived her emotional and physical traumas with a Satanic cult and released each experience, one by one.

If you are ready to explore a method that mankind has been searching and praying for, a process in which some have claimed their hearts have felt His Presence while falling into God's Arms, then please check out this wonderful procedure.

Classes are being formed daily. Please call 713-784-7440 for information or 1-800-645-7991 to order Green Magic Food Supplement.

Taraisms

Taraisms and Words of Wisdom are just that, a list of quotes and words that I live by. The Taraisms are Universally composed. The Words of Wisdom are by various authors. These empowering phrases are scattered throughout the book for you to find. "Seek and ye shall find."

1. Change is necessary.
2. Have faith and trust in the Divine.
3. Perfection in, perfection out.
4. Go within to find your truths
5. Unconditional love stops fear.
6. Intention is a map for the mind.
7. Change is good when it's apparent.
8. A sense of humor makes good sense.
9. Love is the driving force of the soul.
10. The cure for lying is telling the truth.
11. Denial is a veil to the conscious mind.
12. Do it now and the world surrounds you.
13. If it's not easy and effortless, don't do it!
14. You don't see because you are not looking.
15. A massage is a message of love to the body.
16. When one goes within, one is never without.
17. Face your obstacles with full empowerment.
18. There is always a lesson within lessons.
19. Friends always in need are pests; let them go!
20. Understanding the past is a lifeline to a happier future.
21. When you open your heart, you soar like an eagle.
22. I am one, you are one, but we can be one together.
23. You are what you say, think, feel, believe and eat.
24. Unresolved issues remain as painful experiences.
25. Healing the past is necessary to fulfill your destiny.
26. Selflessness is not selfishness; serve yourself first.
27. We are always guided to the people we need to meet.

28. Go within and find comfort from life's daily escalators.
29. If you stay in the shadows, you will remain in the dark.
30. The power of love surpasses all in a time of indecision.
31. What you dislike the most will come back and defeat you.
32. When you listen to your body, it will tell you what it needs.
33. If you don't know how to spell success how can you succeed?
34. Life is unkind to those stuck in the unhappiness from the past.
35. Allowing yourself to be happy is better than having to be right.
36. Heal the past, live in the now and the future is yours to command.
37. The Universe will support you when you put your intentions out into the Cosmos.
38. When you remember what you were brought here to do, you will do what you want to do, and be who you want to be.
39. When you open your heart and bring in those for your Highest Good, you allow the healing to take place.
40. If it doesn't feel good in your heart, your adult barometer, don't do it!
41. Your subconscious is the hidden, closeted, storehouse to all your secrets.
42. There is an unknown force within us waiting for the spark to ignite the wisdom that would be our life's work.
43. Allow yourself to see behind your realm of understanding and you will know peace of mind.
44. Surround yourself with those on the path of enlightenment.
45. Do it and the money comes; not, I'll do it when the money comes.
46. It doesn't matter why people act out; it's how you react that is important.
47. Always be prepared to come from love and understanding, no matter what the situation.
48. Heal the past, live in the now, and all will come to pass.
49. It doesn't matter if you don't understand the cause of your distress, just be willing to let it go.
50. No matter what we learn and experience along life's highways and byways; everything happens in divine order.

51. Whenever anything happens, no matter how small, large or devastating, it all happens for a reason.
52. Know that when we ask for help from The Universal Realm, we are never alone.
53. Replacing hate and fear with Love and Light has changed many an incarcerated being.
54. Creating a vacuum helps bring in more purposeful people, places and things.
55. Unburdening hate, the opposite of Love, and replacing it with Love and Light, will not take long.
56. No one really does anything to you. They are your teachers pushing your buttons from a past not yet resigned.
57. Your first thought is the true connection to your Higher Self or the Astral plane.
58. Negative energy will stay within the body unless you are willing to let it go.
59. Even in adversity a Light comes forth to show you the way.
60. When a dis-ease is not resolved in the emotional, it will then manifest into a physical disease.
61. Allow yourself to release that which keeps you from your Higher State of Consciousness.
62. When one is ready to release any harmful tendencies, the recovery is swift and painless.
63. Unresolved experiences are situations in your life which you are unable to cope with.
64. When I walk down the corridors of life's grand rewards, I know no bounds.
65. You are the problem and the captain of your fate.
66. Now, when I open my heart, I only bring in those who are for my Highest Good and soul growth.
67. It is the unhappy inner child that lashes out in confusion from an unresolved past.
68. A coincidence is The Universal Connection to our Spiritual Guidance whenever we ask for help.
69. Whenever you think you are controlling a situation you are really out of control.

70. We are not smart enough to make up the feelings and messages from Universal Spirit Guides; trust those first Cosmic answers.

71. If you feel you are being hurt or taken advantage of in any way, immediately put an end to their control and take back your power.

72. Addiction is a two way street; a give and take, or the 'blind addict leading the blind.'

73. Not all that is seen by the naked eye is gospel in the all knowing Spiritual Realm.

74. Running away does not get you anywhere; facing your obstacles will.

75. Stop your endless searching for answers outside yourself.

76. Focus your attention on healing the past and all will manifest in Divine Order.

77. Stay in the now and live your purposeful life to the fullest.

78. Nobody or anything can incite you unless there are unresolved issues attached to an unhappy memory or action.

79. When you open your heart and bring in those for your Highest Good; you allow the healing to take place.

80. If you are not completely in touch with your emotional problems, they will manifest into dis-ease.

81. When an uncomfortable incident is not 'nipped in the bud' it skyrockets into a continuous fear throughout your life.

82. You are a perfect Child of God, destined to do great things.

83. Even through adversity, comes a Light to show you the way.

84. When you are through being part of the school of 'hard-knocks,' join the school of "God-knocks" and all will be opened unto you.

85. Knowing why you are doing what you do, leads you to finding your answers.

86. When you allow your healing to take place, you are free and open to bring in a partner for your Highest Good.

87. Releasing all negativity is the pathway to freedom.

88. Love can move mountains and change all mistrust, hostilities and fear.

89. Come to us with your broken wings and learn to fly free.

90. There are unknown hidden stories calling for explanations within our family madness.
91. Listen and you shall receive.
92. Replace unwanted messages with positive ones.
93. Running away does not get you anywhere; facing your obstacles will.
94. A situation, problem, pain, or emotional upset appears to help us look at and understand what is really going on in our lives.
95. When in doubt surrender; give it up and let it go.
96. There are no secure spaces while you are still living in an addicted existence.
97. When an owner uses an animal's love in place of a human's, a deep feeling of loss and emotional devastation can ensue after the animal dies.
98. We are all co-conspirators in life's emotional plays.
99. Change your toxic eating habits before they are catapulted from your "open mouth insert food receptacle," creating an eating disorder.
100. It does not take long for the give and take of karmic action to occur when you are willing to open to this Cosmic way of life.
101. When we let go of the past we are free to move on.
102. Ask yourself, "Am I now ready and willing to release all the negative thoughts and unwanted energy that may not be for my Highest Good?"
103. Love means Let Our Voice Express.

Appendix 4
Words of Wisdom

1. Ego means, "Edging God Out."
2. Emotion is energy in action.
3. Everything happens in divine order.
4. What you dare to dream of, dare to do.
5. Love is the way I walk in gratitude.
6. No one can hurt you without your permission.
7. Unresolved emotions create disease within the body.
8. We bring into our life that which we fear the most.
9. It's OK to get paid for what you enjoy doing the most.
10. It's okay to say no without hurting peoples' feelings, and it's okay for them to say no to you without hurting your feelings.
11. Praying is talking to God. Meditating is listening to God.
12. Whenever you learn, it's always positive.
13. To conquer others is to have power; to conquer yourself is to know the way.
14. If you want to move, you have to know when to pack.
15. When you don't know what to do, and you're going in circles, do something.
16. Unless you change a negative into a positive, it will remain a negative.
17. A gift is not a gift when there are strings.
18. For knowledge to be useful it must be applied.
19. If we do not heal the past we are forced to repeat it.
20. Nothing is good or bad, only as it relates to YOU!
21. Have faith and look to the Divine.
22. Fear is an acronym for "False Evidence Appearing Real"
23. To believe, you need not understand.
24. When you are ready, the teachers come or you will seek them out.
25. Some have stated that our existence is like the game of Life. I chose to see life as the games or lessons we play out, since we are all "God's Winning Children" — We All Win At Life.

More Words of Wisdom

A Russian saying:
May angels appear at your doorstep!

Creating happiness
Negative thinking is a protection against disappointment. A negative thinker expects nothing good to happen so they are not disappointed when it doesn't.
1. If you like a thing, enjoy it without guilt or fear.
2. If you don't like it, avoid it: job, person, food or place.
3. If you don't like it, but can't avoid it, change it.
4. If you don't like it, can't avoid it, and can't change it, accept it. Accept by changing the viewpoint.

Affirmation from a Unity Church service folder:
I willingly let go of all limiting thoughts and unite my mind and heart with Your divine ideas of wholeness, abundance and love. I am now an open vessel to receive Your rich and infinite blessings. My thoughts, feelings and actions are the instruments of God's.

Affirmations towards the purpose in your life
(Unknown source)

I have a positive viewpoint towards myself.
Every day I get more and more confident in my ability
to direct myself.
Every day I get better and better to take control of my life.
Every day I get better and better to be what I want to be.
Every day I get better and better at doing what I want to do.
Therefore, I feel better and better and better!

Prosperity Affirmations:
1. Money is my friend.
2. I now have plenty of money.
3. Prosperity is my birthright.

4. Life rewards me with abundance.
5. My income now exceeds my expenses.
6. It is now safe to surpass my parents.
7. Abundance is mine by Divine right.
8. I enjoy being economically self-sufficient. It is OK for me to exceed my goals.
9. The Divine plan of my life is now manifest. I don't have to work hard to get money.
10. I now have a success consciousness with money.
11. I have the right to give myself permission to be wealthy.
12. I deserve to be wealthy, rich, prosperous, and affluent.
13. If I get out of the way, money will drop into my lap.
14. Each year my money increases faster than I can spend it.
15. I now have prosperity consciousness all the time.
16. Whenever I seem to lose, a bigger win is on the way.
17. People enjoy paying me money for what I enjoy doing the most.
18. I give thanks that I Am appropriately clothed, housed and transported with the rich substance of God.
19. Divine intelligence shows me all I need to know.
20. Let Divine health manifest for me and in me now.
21. All my words are charged with prospering power.
22. This is a time of Divine completion.

Affirmations by Katherine Ponder that are found in my prosperity bags to teach prosperity consciousness and create money. The first time I used these, $400 appeared in my checking account!

1. Money, money, money manifest thyself here and now in rich abundance.
2. Everything and everybody prospers me now.
3. I thank you (wherever the money will be coming from, a job, person, etc.) and I thank God for the riches that are being demonstrated in an through you. So be it. Praise God.

Say each sentence individually 3 times and end it with, So be it. Praise God.

Appendix 6
Liver Cleanse

This is a liver cleanse to help release built up gravel and stones that can block the ducts causing many problems, including the removal of your gall bladder. Perform this necessary cleanse at least twice a year.

Ingredients: 24 ounces water, 6 ounces virgin olive oil, the juice from 1 large fresh pink grapefruit, 4 Tablespoons Epsom salt, glasses.

Dissolve Epsom salt in water; pour 4 ounces in each of the glasses and refrigerate. Have a liquid breakfast (smoothie or juice from organic carrots and 1 apple), nonfat lunch and no food after 2 p.m.

At 6 p.m., drink the first glass of water. At 8 p.m., the second glass and at 10 p.m. take the third glass. Next, blend the olive oil and grapefruit juice; drink 3 ounces and go to sleep.

At 6 a.m., drink fourth glass of water; the fifth glass at 8 a.m. and the sixth at 10 a.m. Drink the second glass of juice at 12 noon; eat a salad for lunch and a light supper.

This combination will open the liver so it can release the waste that continually builds up as calcium deposits and other debris that can not pass through the body, without help or surgery, as kidney stones do.

You will be astonished by how many different sized stones that will come pouring out. It may take half the day to complete, so you may wish to let go on a weekend or when you have a day to *release what you no longer need in your life both physically and mentally*. You might want to say that during the cleanse.

Remember, the liver and gall bladder have to do with being stuck.

To order more copies of **Universe On The Move**
mail copies of this form to:

Angel Heart Publishing

2923 Crossview, Ste B-11 • Houston, TX 77063-4215
or call 713-784-7440
Please make checks payable to: Tara A. Rae

Ship to:

Name: _____

Address: _____

City, State, Zip: _____

Phone: _____ Fax: _____

Special instructions: (Pease print)

Shipping and handling is $4 (minimum) per order or 8% of the total book price.
We use priority mail when sending 1-3 books, UPS Ground with 4 or more.

_____ copies of *Universe On The Move* at $15.95 each = _____

Shipping = _____

Texas residents please add   Tax (if applicable) = _____

8¼% Texas sales tax

Total = _____

Also available from Tara Rae:
Harmony Balancing Bracelets ($25-35)
Harmony Balancing Necklaces ($45-55)
Each is custom made for you. Each contains a variety
of gemstones and crystals. Ask about the **Prosperity
Bag ($12)** containing nine stones and affirmations
that you teach prosperity consciousness.
To discuss your harmony balancing
call Tara Rae at 713-784-7440.